Acknowledgements

The transcripts contained in this volume have been taken from copies of the 'Hamilton Advertiser' of the period, and are reproduced by kind perm
Mr John Rowbotham.

The valued co-operation of staff, Hamilton Library Reference and Local History Department, Town House, Almada Street, Hamilton is also gratefully acknowledged.

Dedication

This collection of Strathaven news of the period 1914 - 1918 is dedicated to the men of the Parish of Avondale and Strathaven who made the supreme sacrifice in The First World War

And to those who came after them in the Second World War 1939 - 1945.

"The died that we might live."

"Age shall not weary them, nor the years condemn, at the going down of the sun and in the morning we will remember them."

Foreword

Like so many others, I found myself fascinated by the political intrigue and secret deals that resulted in the First World War and its catastrophic consequences for the continent of Europe and the world at large. The 'Great War' touched the lives of people in every hamlet, village, town and city worldwide. Readers will already be familiar with the historic events of the many battles of the Western Front stalemated by trench warfare. However, few Stravonian's alive today will have much in the way of knowledge concerning the pace of life here on the Home Front. It was for this reason I decided to research and share with a wider public Strathaven's news columns of the period as published week-on-week in the "Hamilton Advertiser". They provide a unique snapshot of everyday life in Strathaven as the community grappled with the effects of total war and social change while simultaneously seeking to maintain local traditions. It occurred to me that Stravonian's old and new would welcome this opportunity to share a glimpse of the everyday life of the community throughout those turbulent years that marked a major turning point in the history of Strathaven and the world at large.

The years 1914 - 1918 are epitomised in epithets such as The Great War, The Great War for Civilization, and the war to end all wars which, together, encapsulate The First World War. This conflict was not only the first world war, it was also the world's first industrial war. This was the conflict that introduced an unsuspecting world to the horrors of scientific warfare with its use of poison gas, submarine warfare on the high seas and aerial bombardment of towns, cities, railroads and industry across continental Europe. The German invasion of neutral Belgium sent an estimated one and a half million refugees fleeing across the border into the Netherlands, France and across the North Sea to Britain. Approximately 325,000 refugees sought refuge in France, slightly over 160,000 came to Britain, and about 100,000 lived in the Netherlands until the end of the war. Of the 160,000 Belgian refugees who fled to Britain, some 2000 found safe-haven in Scotland. Of these, some 140 families , including members of the Vanderheyden family, were billeted in Strathaven under the care of the Belgian Refugee Committee in association with The City of Glasgow Corporation. That the people of Strathaven opened their doors and their hearts to warmly receive them is recalled by Mr. Jean-Pierre Vercruysse of Belgium whose grandmother constantly exhorted him to never forget the name Strathaven, and the names which came forward most were those of Reverend and Mrs Dey of Rankin U.F. Church.

In Retrospect

At the outbreak of the war, declared on 4 August, 1914, the crowned heads of Britain, Russia, Germany and the Austro-Hungarian empire all sat firmly on their thrones. However, with the murder of Czar Nicholas 11, his wife and family, in the cellar of the 'Ipatiev' mansion, the sinister House of Special Purpose, at Ekaterinberg in the Urals, at the hands of the Bolsheviks in 1918, the revolution in Russia utterly crushed czarism. That year also witnessed the abdication of the German Kaiser Wilhelm II who, having sought and obtained political asylum in neutral Holland, lived the rest of his life at Doorn. The Austro-Hungarian Emperor Franz Joseph was already dead and his once proud Austro-Hungarian empire broken up and parcelled-out among the emerging new nations created when the map of Europe was redrawn at the Paris Peace Conference in 1919 that ratified the signing of the Armistice on 11 November, 1918. The key players at the Peace Conference in Versailles in 1919 were the leaders of Great Britain, France, Italy and the United States who excluded Germany's leaders from these negotiations. The Treaty of Versailles, held Germany to have been wholly responsible for the war. Consequently, Germany was made to suffer the loss of Alsace-Lorraine, her colonies, and to bear the overwhelming burden of the cost of the war set-out in a raft of reparations that bankrupted her, gave rise to runaway inflation, and resulted in the fall of the Weimar Republic. History has taught us that the effects of the Treaty of Versailles on Germany nurtured the rise of Nazism and Adolf Hitler. The world at large knows the outcome of that painful history. Significantly, as a consequence of The First World War, and the rise of Communism, the world would never be the same. At the outset of the war Britain relied on its standing army of volunteers for defence of the realm. However, recruitment swung into action with Lord Kitchener's recruitment poster playing a vital role in touching the British sense of 'fair-play' and patriotism, and deep sense of indignation at Germany's 'rape of little Belgium.' Kitchener's finger pointed accusingly from the poster above a caption that read: 'Your Country Needs You!' This and Britain's initial defeat at the Battle of Mons (a retreat that was claimed a victory) did the trick. Within days, rather than weeks, thousands upon thousands of men and boys had answered 'The Call' to serve 'God, King and Country'. The people of Britain were led to believe that it would all be over by Christmas. The Hun would be defeated and everything would be back to normal. There have been innumerable accounts of the atrocities and casualties of the war in the trenches and in the many battles that ended in stalemate along a Western front stretching 600 miles from France all the way to Switzerland. Britain paid a terrible price in terms of 9 million lives lost. However, Britain's Tommies held the line and served with valour. The names of many of the lads who left Strathaven to fight in that war never to return are named among the casualties listed in the Hamilton Advertiser of the period and subsequently inscribed on Strathaven's War Memorial and the Rolls of Honour erected and preserved within the several churches of the town. Amidst the horror of life in the trenches the Strathaven lads eagerly awaited letters and parcels of home comforts and, not least, their copy of the Hamilton Advertiser sent by their loved ones. One can guess the excitement generated when a copy of that newspaper arrived from home. In reading this news from the Home Front they, like us, could hardly fail to have been struck by the fact that back here in Strathaven things were going along much as before, except for the fact that their was a great deal of fund-raising in aid of the war effort. Otherwise, the local events recorded are not all that different from those that inform Strathaven readers of the Hamilton Advertiser a century later.

Bob Currie

Strathaven

2010.

Hamilton Advertiser

Issue; Saturday, 3rd January, 1914.

Calendars:

Mr Campbell, Ironmonger, Commongreen, has again issued his calendar in the form of a wall pocket with monthly tabs attached to the bottom. On the flap of the pocket is a very good photo of Mr & Mrs Campbell taken at their exhibitions stand, which is usually one of the features of the annual cattle show. The calendar will be found both useful and ornamental.

Mr Samuel W. Gilmour's issue is a long hanger with a pretty print of the picture "Motherless". The picture is "quiet" and delicate and will lend charm to the walls of any room.

Soup Kitchen:

The festive season has not been forgotten by the promoters and friends of this public charity. On Christmas Day, the Rev. Mr Donaldson provided a special treat for the children, in the shape of extra well filled bags of buns and pastries, along with which they each received a large sized picture-card appropriate to the occasion. On the last day of the old year, they were kindly served with a bag of sweets by Mrs Lusk, and with an orange by Mrs Mason; and on New Year's Day, by the continued generosity of Mr Murray of Low Ploughland, they got the usual substantial mutton pies made from the sheep annually gifted by him for this purpose.

Hastie Trust:

We are pleased to be able to announce that negotiations have been completed by the Hastie Trust for the purchase of that ground to the rear of Green Street and Lethame Road known as Grierson's Holm. Since games are not allowed in the George Allan Public Park it is probable that this new public park may be set aside exclusively for games, and in doing so the Trustees will be acting quite in compliance with the Will of the late Mr Hastie, which indicated a recreation ground. The park is nicely situated along the course of the Pomillion, and its adaptability for games is borne out by the fact that it was at one time the ground of the Vale of Avondale Football Club. Between this ground and the present public park a portion of the Glebe intervenes, and already the Trustees are making inquiries with a view to purchasing sufficient of this ground to form a connection link between the two parks.

Issue: Saturday. 10th January, 1914.

Burns:

An effort is again being made to resuscitate a night which in former times was the night of the social season for the commemoration of our national poet's birthday, and already arrangements are well forward for the revival. Dr. Mason has promised to deliver the oration, and everything points to a successful gathering. See advert.

Series of Lectures:

In connection with the Christadelphian Ecclesia, the first of a series of lectures was given in the Good Templar Hall on Sunday evening by Mr Mullin, his subject being "Socialism, or the reign of Christ upon Earth." There was a good attendance, and the lecture was much enjoyed. Tomorrow evening Mr Sam. C. Cavin will speak on "When the land shall bring forth its increase." See advert.

Novel Competition:

For the purpose of raising funds, the Vale of Avon Amateur Football Club recently issued subscription sheets for the collection of 1d donations. Each subscriber's name was entered against an hour, minute and second on the sheets. About a fortnight ago a gold watch was purchased, wound, and put away in a safe. When all the sheets had come in the watch was taken from the safe and the competitor whose name was opposite the exact second at which it had stopped had the option of purchasing the watch for 1/-. The gentleman who proved the winner was Mr J. B. Cochran c/o Messrs. Arthur & Company, Glasgow.

Issue: Saturday, 17th January, 1914.

Warning to Boys:

Complaint has been made for some time by the officials at the Central Station of boys and young men trespassing in the Goods Yard and other premises of the company, and playing games etc., on Sundays. On Sunday last the police were on the watch, and we understand that 2 youths were caught, and that they will probably be brought up in Court in due course.

Issue: Saturday, 31st January,. 1914.

Illustrated Lecture:

There was a good attendance in the Salvation Army Hall on Wednesday evening, when Adjutant Thomas Bloss, a Canadian officer, gave a most interesting lecture entitled "The Call of the British Colonies." The country principally dealt with was Canada, regarding which the Adjutant asserted there were exceptionally fine prospects for pushing young people. A large series of very interesting pictures was thrown on the screen, the operator being Ensign Halliday of the Glasgow Emigration Department. Mr James M. Bryson presided.

Avondale Ploughing Society:

The annual competition of the society was held yesterday in a field on the farm of Righead, kindly granted for the purpose by the tenant, Mr Peter McFarlane. On account of the unfavourable weather the number of competitors was not up to former years, but notwithstanding that, the keenest rivalry for the highest honours in all the classes took place, the work performed being of a high-class character.

Burns Celebration:

The second annual supper of the poet's admirers in Strathaven was held on Friday evening 23rd inst., in Mr Robertson's Hall, Waterside Street, the company being only limited by the meeting capacity of the hall. There can be no doubt that by another year a Burns' Club will be resuscitated and the past glories of the anniversary meeting revived.

Issue: Saturday, 21st February, 1914.

Marriage Celebration - Crown Hotel:

The marriage was celebrated in the Crown Hotel on Wednesday of Mr Alexander Meikle, The Ferme, Glassford, and Miss Helen Mair, only daughter of the late James and Mrs Kemp, Crown Hotel. The ceremony took place in the hall, which has been in the hands of the decorators for some days and the arrangement with flowers, screens etc., was exceptionally pretty. The bride was dressed in cream satin charmeuse with pearl embroidery and point lace, veil sewn with lovers' knots and court train lined with pink chiffon. She carried a sheaf of earn lilies, orange blossom and maiden hair ferns. The bridesmaids, Misses McWhannel, Mary Kemp, and Bessie Fisher were dressed in white satin with mob cap and touches of pink. They carried bouquets of pink and white tulips. Mr Thomas Frew was groomsman. The service was fully choral - Mr R. A. Fleming presiding at the organ. Rev. John Muirhead, B.D., minister of Avondale Parish Church, officiated, assisted by the Rev. Robert Paterson, M.A., Glassford Parish Church. The bride was given away by her mother, who was beautifully gowned in amethyst silk embroidered with violets and cream lace. She wore a Tagel hat with wreath of forget-me-nots and upstanding osprey, and sable furs. Immediately after the ceremony a reception was held. At five o'clock the young couple went away by motor, the bride wearing a blue and orange frock, with hat to match, musquash coat and Persian lamb muff. Later in the evening the guests were driven by motor to Glasgow to attend theatre. A magnificent array of presents was received by the bride.

Issue: Saturday, 28th February, 1914.

Sudden Death:

Annie Coats (42), spinster was found dead in the grip in the byre at Crosshill Farm at 6.15 pm on Saturday last. The deceased woman, who was a sister of the farmer, had been engaged in milking the cows. Twice she came into the house to empty her pails, and as she seemed long in coming back for the third time Mrs Coats went into the byre to see what was detaining her, and to her horror found her sister-in-law lying dead on the floor. At five o'clock the household had taken tea together, and at that time Miss Coats appeared to be in her usual good health, and was particularly cheery. It was at first supposed that she had been kicked by a cow, but examination failed to reveal any marks on her body, and Dr. Alan Watt, who was hastily summoned gave it as his opinion that death was due to heart failure.

Bell Ringers:

The earlier hour of bell-ringing begins on 1st March, and we are informed the Bell Ringer has arranged to ring at 5 am, instead of at 5.30 as formerly. This alteration will be appreciated by workmen who travel by the workman's train at 5.35 as it will give them 35 minutes notice, whereas under the old arrangement they had only 5 minutes.

War Against Consumption:

Under the auspices of the Insurance Committee for the County of Lanark, Dr. J. R. Currie, medical officer to the Scottish Insurance Commissioners, gave a lecture on the above subject in the Public Hall on Monday evening. Mr James Cameron, C.E., C.C., presided. Aided by a series of good illustrations, thrown on the screen by a powerful lantern, the doctor made the lecture most homely and interesting. Dealing first of all with the question:- What is consumption? He described the various forms, with an explanation of the probable cause of contraction, he then proceeded to describe how the disease should be treated; and where no indication had yet arisen, how the disease was to be avoided. Dr. Currie laid great emphasis on the fact that the sun, fresh air, and good food were the enemies of the bacilli of consumption, and urged the audience to avail themselves to the very utmost of these things so convenient to their hand, Too confined sleeping accommodation and too many rugs, etc., about a room also came in for condemnation. By a series of diagrams the progress in the fight against consumption was illustrated, and these gave great cause to believe that with modern knowledge and appliance the disease may yet, and before long, be practically exterminated. Mr W. M. Marshall, Clerk of the County Insurance Committee, made a few remarks re the work done by the committee since the introduction of the Insurance Act in July, 1912. Over 200 cases had been treated.

Jubilee Services:

As will be seen from our advertising column, the Rev. John Young, late of Greenock, is to preside in the East United Free Church on Sabbath forenoon. On Tuesday evening, in same place, the jubilee of the ministry of Rev. Alexander W. Donaldson, B.A., will be celebrated with fitting ceremonial.

The Late Mr James H. Alston:

The news of the death of Mr Alston in Glasgow on Wednesday reached Strathaven about four o'clock, and caused widespread regret. Mr Alston had gone into Glasgow on business feeling quite his usual, and when in West George Street, collapsed on the pavement. An ambulance wagon was summoned to take him to the Royal Infirmary, but before that institution was reached Mr Alston had passed away. On account of his connection with the Auction Mart Limited, of which he was secretary and treasurer, his fame as one of the leading exponents; of shorthand , and his great ability (for a number of years he acted as our Strathaven correspondent) Mr Alston was one of the best known men in the district. During the earlier part of his career the deceased was a reporter in the Law Courts in London. He had been editor of the phonetic magazine, and was examiner on that subject to the Glasgow Athenaeum. One of the greatest works he has done was the preparation of the lithographic transfers for the Bible in Shorthand, published by Messrs. Isaac Pitman & Sons. Not only in shorthand did he excel, for there was no more beautiful writer and pen artist to be found than he. The latter acquirement was splendidly demonstrated in several illuminated addresses he has done in recent times. An early member of the Mutual Improvement Association, he has followed the fortunes of that body practically during the whole course of its career. There were few subjects introduced that he could not go into, sometimes exhibiting amazing knowledge of intricate questions. Nor did he confine himself to the M.I.A., for the Literary Society of the West United Free Church, of which he was a member, had the good fortune to possess him as their vice-president. Not long ago Mr Alston prepared a paper on Maeterlinck's "Bluebird" which was delivered at the M.I.A., and those competent to judge declared it to be a masterpiece. Mr Alston was a great Burnsonian, and was mainly responsible for the original Burns' Club in Strathaven. When that club had been in abeyance for some years, it fell to him, some three years ago, to be the reorganiser. A man of quiet and unassuming manner, his modesty carried him to the point of bashfulness. There was no self-advertising about the man, but when one had the privilege of knowing him personally they realised they had become acquainted with a man of great merit and ability, a strong friend and an ideal companion. He leaves a widow to whom the heartfelt sympathy of the community goes out in her great sorrow.

Issue: Saturday, 14th March, 1914.

Honour to Local Baker:

We observe with pleasure that Mr Daniel H. Taylor, baker, common green, has been amongst the prize winners at the annual bakers and confectioners exhibition, held at Edinburgh during the week. The award is a silver medal (2nd place) for Scotch bun.

Issue: Saturday, 21st March, 1914.

New Caledonian Stationmaster:

Mr William Twaddle, Ryeland and Drumclog Station, has been appointed the new Caledonian stationmaster at Lugton. His successor at Ryeland and Drumclog is Mr Samuel Patrick.

Parish Council of Avondale:

In the report of the Council meeting last week the name of "Wyper" should have been "Wynn", and the bequest referred to was Miss Gebbie's. The bequest which is very much appreciated is one of £100 handed in trust to the Parish Council in 1904, the interest being distributed annually to 5 parishioners in terms of Miss Gebbie's instructions.

Issue: Saturday, 28th March, 1914.

Housebreaking:

The Tavern public house in Hamilton Road was broken into between Friday and Saturday of last week. Fortunately there was not much money about, and the burglar had to be content with the rather cumbersome haul of 8s in coppers which had been laid in for Sunday use. A man is in custody in connection with the affair, and it is believed that he is the perpetrator of quite a series of robberies that have taken place within an are of some 15 miles.

Issue: Saturday, 4th April, 1914.

Warning to Boys:

At the J.P. Court, Hamilton, on Thursday, five respectably dressed lads were charged with creating a breach of the peace on Threestanes Road near the George Allan Park, on the night of Sunday, 22nd March. They pleaded guilty, and were admonished.

Issue: Saturday, 11th April, 1914.

Clothes Washing Demonstration:

On Tuesday last our town had a specimen of up-to-date methods of advertising. Mr James P. Morrison, ironmonger, Commongreen, having procured the agency for the "Swift" Vacuum Washer, arranged a demonstration of the machine in the Public Hall. A large number of ladies and some gentlemen took advantage of the invitation given in the local press to witness what the machine could do to alleviate the labour of "blue" Monday. An expert demonstrator was in attendance, and amply proved that the machine could do more than is claimed for it. The advantages of the "Swift" washer are so obvious that in the words of one of the ladies present, no common sense housewife should be without one. The washer is sold locally by Mr James P. Morrison at the reasonable sum of 14s.6d.

Issue: Saturday, 18th April, 1914.

An Avondale Columnist - Prosperous Merchant in Rhodesia:

Mr John Meikle, merchant of Umtali, Rhodesia, was born at Strathaven in 1868. Going out to South Africa while a youth, he proceeded in 1892 to Rhodesia, where he is a very successful and prominent colonist. He is the youngest of the three brothers Meikle whose business operations extend from one end of the territory to the other. He takes a keen interest in farming and arboriculture, and his "Mountain Home" contains some of the finest plantations in Rhodesia. Mr Meikle was a member of the Rhodesia Legislative Council in 1903-04. He stood at the recent General Election as anti-Charter candidate for the Eastern Division. The polling took place on March 18th, and resulted in Mr Meikle's defeat, in company, it should be said, with the defeat of all the other anti-Charter candidates in the country. Mr Meikle's successful opponent was Mr Lionel Cripps, an Umtali farmer, who polled 317 votes as against 260 cast for Mr Meikle.

The Late :Mr John Alston:

We have received the following for publication: - *"Philadelphia, U.S.A. - We. The Strathaven natives living in Philadelphia, were deeply grieved to read in the columns of the "Hamilton Advertiser" of the death of our dear friend, Mr J. H. Alston, and we should be failing in the great obligation we owe his memory if we did not convey our deepest sympathy to our fellow-townsmen in the great loss they have sustained. Our hearts go out in sympathy also to Mrs Alston in her great grief. He was loved by those who knew him best. - J. B. W."*

Cycling Accident:

A rather serious accident befell a man named William Whiteford (34) engineman, of Swinhill, whilst cycling home from Strathaven on Friday evening last. Near Netherfield Lodge he seemed to lose control of his bicycle and fell on the side of the road. Charles Dunn of Netherburn, who accompanied Whiteford, did what he could for him, and a Strathaven man coming along hurried into town and notified Dr. Mason. After being attended to by the latter, the unfortunate man was conveyed home by motor, and has not at time of writing (Thursday evening) recovered consciousness. The nature of his injury is concussion of the brain.

Issue: Saturday, 9th May, 1914.

The Palace of Delight:

"The Palace of Delight" Dr. Machardy's latest comic opera, is to be performed on Tuesday first in the Public Hall. It is full of fun, and contains many Scottish characteristics, and several of the finest Scottish airs are interwoven in the work. Dr Machardy (whose life's work has been to raise Scottish music to a high place in the rank of musical works) appeals to his countrymen to come and hear his opera. We hope he will receive a gratifying response to his appeal in the shape of a large audience. Rev. John Muirhead will occupy the chair and address the audience upon the patriotic musical work Dr. Machardy is doing for this country.

Celebration of Coming of Age:

To celebrate the coming of age of his son Thomas, Mr John Bryce Buchanan, late of West Browncastle, gave an "At Home" in the Royal Oak Hall, Paisley, on Tuesday, 21st ult. Mr Alexander Taylor, Allerstocks, occupied the chair. During the course of the evening Mr William Henderson, on behalf of the Churchill Club, presented the young man with a magnificent gold hunter watch, ribbon and seal. The latter part of the evening was devoted to dancing, and at intervals songs were well rendered by members of the party. Mr Buchanan has been the recipient of a large number of presents from other sources in honour of the occasion.

Issue: Saturday, 16th May, 1914.

Strathaven Golf Club:

Mr William Allan, of Elderslie, the president of the club, will open the course for the season today at 3 o'clock. Notwithstanding this formality the golf course is open all the year round, the soil being of such a nature as to permit of play at any time in reasonable weather. It is hoped there will be a good turnout of members and friends today.

Issue: Saturday, 23rd May, 1914.

Of Interest to Farmers:

In an account of the Johannesburg Agricultural Show in South Africa paper to hand this week, we have pleasure in noting that Mr A. S. Atkins has been first and won the championship with the bull "High Drumclog Sir Daniel". This bull was sold to Mr Atkins some time ago by Mr Thomas A Findlay, High Drumclog.

Local View Cards:

Mr John Pinkerton, Commongreen, has added to the already extensive series of local view cards some 30 new views. To have seen the collection previously, one would have concluded that every view in the district worth taking had been secured, and it comes as quite a surprise that the views now published are practically all new and many of them not previously seen, as for instance - view of Lochar, Shoogly Brig and Primrose Braes, Hapton Crags, R.C. Chapel and Manse, Meeting of Kype and Avon, Meeting of Holburn and Avon, etc., while some old favourites are revived in the Big Lime (Kype), Loudon Hill, and so on. The new list are all of the "glossy" description in various tints, and make a fine addition to an already elaborate series.

Issue: Saturday, 11th June, 1914.

Factory Act Prosecution:

In Hamilton Sheriff Court on Thursday, William Muir, being the occupier of a workshop at 11 Barn Street, Strathaven, pleaded guilty to having contravened the above Act on 16th May, in respect that he had employed a young person at 5.25 in the morning. He was fined £1.6s.4d (including expenses) the alternative being 5 days imprisonment.

Cycling Accident:

On Monday, a lad named Robert Thomson lost control of his bicycle coming down the Wellbrae, between Kirk Street and the Commongreen, and ran into the wall of Vicarland Cottage. He was thrown violently against the wall, and got a nasty cut on the head which necessitated stitching. He is now doing well and able to go about.

Issue: Saturday, 27th June, 1914.

Bad Boys:

Two young farm servants named John Hartman and William Goudie, were at the J.P. Court, Hamilton, on Monday fined 7s.6d each with the option of 5 days in prison, for creating a disturbance on Saturday evening.

Fire Brigade:

It may still be "news" to some folk that we have now in our midst a specially trained and fully equipped fire brigade, consisting of 3 members of the Lanarkshire Constabulary stationed here, and 2 civilians. The brigade is part of the system inaugurated within recent times by the County Council in conjunction with the police, and as regards fire drill by the County instructor. Two good photographs of the local men are at present on view in the window of Mr William Wilson, cycle merchant etc., in Main Street - the one showing the men in full uniform, and the other in undress uniform, with their hose barrow and equipment. Sergeant Lamont, the instructor, is on the left of the latter photo.

Rainfall in June:

From the records kept at East Overton House, the rainfall last month amounted to only .67 of an inch which is the lowest rainfall recorded in Strathaven in any one month for over ten years past, with the exception of October, 1906 which showed a total of .66 an inch. In the first five months of this year there was a total rainfall of some 20 inches, which is equivalent in weight to 2000 tons of water to the acre.

Monthly Holiday:

Wednesday was observed as the merchants' monthly holiday, when there was a general closing of business premises. The weather was not at all ideal for outings, there being a cold snap in the wind and rain threatening all day. Nevertheless, there were many travellers, and included in the number was the choir of Avendale Parish Church, who went to Rothesay, and the Avondale Farmers, who went by motor to Queensferry.

A Villa Burglary:

There was considerable excitement in the usually quiet district of Crosshill on Wednesday caused by two male burglars entering the villa known as Shalimar. It appears that the tenants, Mr. Mrs and Miss Hamilton, were away for the day. About half-past twelve a sister-in-law of Mr. Hamilton who lives in Bowling Green Road, happening to be looking towards Shalimar from an upstairs window, was surprised to observe two men enter the house. Somewhat puzzled she went up to Shalimar, calling out a neighbour on the way. Jack Coats from the farm nearby accompanied the women, and looking through the window he observed signs which spoke conclusively of burglary. He accordingly ran into the town for police assistance. Meanwhile the men had taken fright and bolted, via the back garden, through the fields, the grounds of Hermon and then the field again towards Newton Farm. Anticipating the route the burglars intended taking, Constable John Pirie mounted his bicycle and got on ahead of them; then turning towards the town he met the men and affected their arrest. At the Police Station the accused gave the following names; James Wallace, age 33, merchant, 13 Govan Street, Glasgow and John Small, age 22, clerk, 219 Commercial Road, Glasgow. In their possession were found the return halves

of railway tickets to Glasgow, and it is surmised that, knowing it was a local holiday, they had come to Strathaven "to see what was doing." It has since been established that both men are known criminals who have served terms of imprisonment for similar offences. They appeared before the Sheriff at Hamilton on Thursday when they were committed to prison pending further enquiries.

Sunday School Excursions:

The annual trip of Drumclog Kirk School was held on Saturday, 20th June, the place of destination being the pleasant seaside resort of Troon. On arrival good fare was lavishly served in the hall of the Portland Arms. The weather was not on its best behaviour, the day being cloudy, with occasional drops of rain. The general feeling, however, was that in spite of Old Sol's reluctance to make a shine, all had enjoyed a pleasant outing. The number of those present at the trip was 106 - the largest yet recorded for a Drumclog trip. Sports were engaged in on the green at the North Promenade, and many keen competitors were gladdened with the King's portrait in current coin. After having done the sights of the town, a return was made to the festal board about 5.30 p.m., and refreshed again, faces were turned station-wards for the homeward trip. A busy centre was that station; many seemed to have come to Troon that day, no doubt because Drumclog had made it the place of its choice. Before separating, a hearty vote of thanks on the call of the Rev. Mr Beaton, was vociferously given to Mr Findlay, superintendent of the school, the teachers, and all who had carried through the arrangements which were perfect throughout. A quick run was made by the train, leaving at 7.45, and on arrival many happy faces were to be seen disembarking at Drumclog aglow with the ozone breezes and glad with happy memories of the seashore - On the same day the Sabbath Schools of Strathaven had a combined outing to Troon where a very pleasant time was spent. The only S.S. not included in the excursion - Avondale Parish Church - went to Rylandside (Mr. Lindsay's) in carts, machines etc., provided by members of the congregation, and in spite of a rather threatening day, enjoyed themselves.

Closing Day At The Academy:

Friday, the 26th ult., was observed as closing day at the Academy. The Avondale School Board was represented by the chairman, Dr. Mason, Mr. Wilson (convener of the Visiting Committee) and Mr. Black, who all took part in the proceedings. Mr James Barrie (clerk of the Board) was also present. After the distribution of the medals and prizes to the senior scholars, Mr Wilson referred to the remarkable success of the school in the Marshall Trust Bursary competition, and in other examinations. Speaking from knowledge as a member of the Secondary Committee he could testify that the education given in their school up to the intermediate certificate stage, which was all the length they were now permitted to go, was second to none, being thoroughly efficient and up-to-date. Dr. Mason in a few closing words, complimented teachers and scholars upon the results of their labours and intimated that the holidays would extend to Monday morning, the 17th August. The gold medallists for the session are Mary Marjorie Broom and John Stirling, who were awarded the medals annually presented by Lady Griffen and Mr. James Gebbie of Netherfield. The next in order - Mary Russell and Claude Barrie - received handsome book prizes. Mr. Barrie's prizes for proficiency in Latin were won by John Stirling, Mary Marjorie Broom, Robert Park and Nellie Stewart. Out of nine or ten Marshall Bursaries of the annual value of £15 and tenable for at least two years, given as a result of a written examination open to scholars from the various public schools of Lanarkshire (excluding Glasgow, but including Govan), this school has won three, which have been awarded to Miss Marjorie Brown, Mary Russell and John Stirling. In the Marshall £10 Bursary competition John Downie and Herbert McCorkell were each awarded a bursary of £10 tenable for two years. Through the kindness of Mrs Mason, Crofthead Cottage, each pupil of the infant department was made the happy recipient of a toy picture book. The following pupils have obtained the group intermediate certificate:- David B.T. Ballantyne, Claude Barrie, Mary Marjorie Broom, Isabella N. Elliott, Alexander G. Fleming, William S. Fleming, Margaret F. Forrest, Mary P.R. Russell, Thomas H. Shearer, John T. Stirling, and Johanna B. Young.

A Notable Retiral:

In the East United Free Church on Sunday the Rev. Alexander Wilkie Donaldson, B.A., bade farewell to the congregation after a ministry of fifty years, forty-four of which have been passed in Strathaven. There was a large gathering of the congregation, and at the evening diet of worship all the congregations of the town were represented. As indicated, Rev. A.W. Donaldson came to Strathaven forty-four years ago, and during that time he had been a splendid force for good in the community. He served with distinction on the School Board for a number of years, and was prominently associated with every public function of note, as well as with all the religious movements which have taken place within the period. A man of known sympathy, he noted the aimless way in which many girls of the poorer classes spent their evenings, and as far back as 1872 he commenced a Girls' Industrial Class which exists to this day. The work of the class is conducted by an efficient staff of monitors who teach the girls sewing and other useful accomplishments, the garments made during the session being distributed among the members of the class. It will readily be understood that the fundamentals of a good housewife were secured by many a lass in such a class. Nor did he forget the boys, though it was a later period, 1887, that he instituted the Boys' Union. The boys were taught physical drill long before the present educational system had made it part of the curriculum, and lessons in music, reading, etc., were also inculcated. Thrift was encouraged in a savings bank, which paid a small percentage of profit on the youngsters' deposits, the accounts being terminable at will. Looking further afield, the reverend gentleman's heart was touched to see numerous children apparently ill nurtured, and so in poor condition for assimilating the instruction given them at the day school. The outcome of this was the commencing of the soup kitchen in the Mission Hall, where each day during the winter needy children are supplied with a hot meal free of charge. Mr. Donaldson had many admirers in this work, and especially at Christmas time there were special treats when the "Australian mutton" or the "Plewland sheep" arrived. So far as his ministry commended itself to his people may be judged by the enthusiastic manner in which the Jubilee of his ministry was celebrated in the month of March. On that occasion commendatory letters were received, from the end of the earth; and friends and acquaintances were gathered from far and near to do him honour. Testimonials and presentations were showered upon him, and speakers representing every phase of public and religious work bore testimony to his worth as a public servant, a minister, and a man. A phase of Mr Donaldson's character, which seems to have escaped attention amongst the speeches at the Jubilee services, but one which was noticeable to the most casual observer was his beautiful understanding of the meaning of "Pastor". Every member of his flock had a place in his heart, and come joy or tribulation, Mr Donaldson was ever ready to be as one with each individual. Particularly in times of sickness and distress, his attention was most devoted; his own time and comfort counted as naught that he might minister to others. We have not always been able to agree with Mr Donaldson, but we have always been able to admire him as a sincere straightforward, and manly Christian gentleman. Going into retirement, he will be missed in public and church life, but his memory will live, and he will be remembered by what he has done. May the evening of his life be sweet and peaceful.

Unionist Association:

A meeting of the town members of this Association was held in the Lesser Public Hall on Monday last to consider a circular received from the Glasgow Port Committee of the "Help the Ulster Women Committee". Mr John Frew, president of the Association presided. The circular stated - "In view of the very serious state of affairs existing in Ulster and the possibility of matters becoming worse, committees for the West of Scotland have been formed for the purpose of making arrangements for the reception, housing, and care of refugees in the event of civil war breaking out. As Scotland would doubtless be called on to receive a large proportion of those (who would be almost entirely women and children) the committee earnestly appeal through you for offers of assistance in either all, of the following directions - (1) Halls for the purpose of receiving and registering refugees on landing; (2) suitable living accommodation to which refugees may afterwards be removed; (3) as many workers, both male and female, as possible to meet refugees on landing, to conduct them to and attend to them at the reception depots in order that they may be transferred as promptly as possible to their more permanent quarters; (4) clerical assistance for identification and registration; (5) promises to receive and board, free, one or more persons. The committee understand you may have some difficulty in getting into touch with many of your members at this particular time of the year, but the matter is of such importance that every effort should be made to bring it before their notice. The committee would wish to impress the extra gravity of the position and the importance of united action, and leave it with confidence in your hands to make the appeal effectual." The Secretary submitted a letter from Mr Leadbetter, Stobieside, offering assistance in various forms, including provision for the board and lodging of four refugees, and he also intimated a promise on somewhat similar lines from Mr and Mrs Lee Dykes, East Overton. Several gentlemen present intimated their willingness to give assistance in the way of providing board and lodging for refugees and money contributions and it was unanimously decided to instruct the secretary to write the Glasgow Port Committee, undertaking, on behalf of the Association to subscribe a minimum sum of £200 over and above making arrangements for the accommodation of several refugees, this fund to be administered by the local Association. Guarantees amounting to practically £100 were intimated at the meeting. Arrangements were also made for hiring the lower premises of the Victoria Hall as an emergency shelter and one gentleman offered a furnished house. Medical attendance, gratis was also promised. It is expected that when the Landward members of the Association are appealed to, they also will respond generously. Meantime, attention is drawn to the notice in our advertising column, appealing for further offers of assistance.

Issue: Saturday, 11th July, 1914.

King and Queen in Scotland - The Tour Through Lanarkshire:

The itinerary of the royal visit to Lanarkshire on Thursday was Parkhead Forge, Coatbridge, Airdrie, Mauldslie Castle, Wishaw, Motherwell and Hamilton. The mere mention of the group of industrial burghs visited was an earnest of the King's tour - that it is intended as far as is humanly possible to come into touch with the busy populations who mean so much to the industry and prosperity of the realm. The area thus chosen may not have many scenic attractions to offer, and with the exception of Hamilton none of the burghs possessed an inspiring past drawn from the pages of history. Rather did the communities represent the modern spirit of progressive industrialism. As has been said, in no other district in Great Britain probably is there greater diversity or more fortunate dispersion of industry. In the county proper there is a population of some 4000,000 gathered principally in the burghs to be visited and along the royal route. Separate entities these burghs are, though an ever-extending tramway transport is linking them together, thereby giving them an inevitable community of interest. A modern artist, surveying these towns, with their flaming furnaces, their smoking chimney stalks, and mountains of refuse, showing how the bowels of the earth are being searched for their coal and mineral treasures, has suggested for heraldic theme: - "Collier with pick, and chimney belching fire." A glance at the armorial of Lanarkshire, however, is less distressing to sentiment. Its principal elements are derived from the insignia of the house of Hamilton and Douglas. The Douglas heart is prominent, recalling the story of the stout Sir James of Douglas, and connecting present institutions with those old days of chivalry when crusade and tournament and adventure were the things the men of rank fought for. Since that pious act of the good Sir James, guardian of the heart of Bruce on its way to Eastern sepulchre, the symbol of the "Bleeding Heart" has figured in the arms of the Douglas family, and has been borrowed for the county arms. The silver cinque foils which also appear there belong to the Hamilton shield. The motto "Vigilantia" is part of a matriculation which savours of the modern spirit which governs the county administration. History lies deeply embedded in the three wards of Lanarkshire. A fragment of the primeval Caledonian Forest is preserved at Cadzow, within the policies of the Duke of Hamilton, where also roams a herd of the native wild cattle. Roman remains may still be traced in the site of ancient camp or military road. Even Motherwell itself claims to have a bridge built by the Roman legions, carrying Watling Street across the deeply wooded glen of the South Calder Waters. Traditions and legends are strewn everywhere, though perhaps more apparent to the seeing eye of the archaeologist and antiquarian than the begrimed collier or steelworker. Right down the pages of history Lanarkshire can claim her share in the "purple" passages - the heroic deeds of Wallace and Bruce, the Reformation struggle, the fall of Queen Mary of Scots, the grim encounters of the Covenanters. Here, as elsewhere, industry has ruthlessly obliterated historical vestiges from the town and villages. Nomenclature alone in many instances is all that survives from the past. Instead of antiquity, their Majesties were confronted with distinctly modern Coatbridge "the Iron Burgh", Motherwell, "Steelopolis", Hamilton (though sometimes known as the Ducal Burgh) headquarters of the county coalmining industry. At all the towns their Majesties were presented to the burgh and county dignitaries, and a general time of rejoicing was observed. Hamilton alone had the honour of a distinct civic ceremony, the King formally opening the new Municipal Buildings.

At Hamilton Palace:

Elaborate preparations were made at Hamilton Palace for the reception of Their Majesties. The spectacle on Their Majesties arrival was a magnificent one, eclipsing even the memorable scene on the same spot seventy-one years ago, when Alexander the tenth Duke of Hamilton, and Susan Euphemia, Duchess of Hamilton, held a public reception after the marriage of the Marquis of Douglas and Clydesdale their son, to Princess Marie of Baden. Along the central portion of the north front of the Palace a great pavilion was erected with stands at each side for the accommodation of representatives of the County of Lanark and Burgh of Hamilton, present by special invitation. The canopy of the pavilion was concealed with intermingling draperies of white and blue, and decorated in front with flags and armorial shields on a ground of blue and gold, the Corinthian columns and sculptured pediment of the Palace giving to all a classical background. To the right of the pavilion was assembled on a special stand 400 members of the Lanarkshire Voluntary Aid Detachment including Red Cross nurses in the distinctive uniform of their profession, while accommodated on the same stand, in recognition, no doubt, of the necessary duties performed by their association on this notable occasion were the wife's of the County and Burgh Police to the number of 200. On another stand to the left the employees on the Hamilton Estates numbering nearly 800 had the opportunity of viewing the brief ceremonies of the afternoon. Both these stands were situated at an angle which enabled those assembled on them to obtain a full view of the presentation ceremony. Motoring from Motherwell, the Royal Party entered the grounds of Hamilton Palace by the gate at Clyde Bridge, and reached the south front of the Palace at 4.15 o'clock. The arrival of the Royal car was the signal for a spontaneous and enthusiastic outburst of welcome which was renewed as Their Majesties stepped on to the covered platform and into their seats on three fine old oak chairs placed in the centre of the carpeted floor. Beside the King and Queen stood Their Majesties retinue: Lady Ampthill (Lady in Waiting), Lady Catherine Hardy, Lord Windborne (Lord in Waiting), Captain the Hon. Sir Charles Fitzwilliam, Vice-Admiral Sir Colin Keppel, and Major Clive Wigram (Equerries).The following Presentation Ceremonies took place:- Representing the Burgh of Hamilton, Provost and Mrs Moffat were presented by His Grace the Duke of Montrose, whereupon Provost Moffat, taking his stand at the right of the King, with Mrs Moffat on the left of the Queen said:- *"Your Majesties I have the honour and pleasure on behalf of the community in extending to Your Majesties a loyal and cordial welcome. I crave Your Majesties permission to present the Town Clerk and the members of the Hamilton Town Council and their wives."* The Burgh representatives were then presented to their Majesties by Provost Moffat in the following order - Mr P.M. Kirkpatrick (town clerk) and Mrs Kirkpatrick. Ex Provost Keith and Mrs Keith. Baillie Brown and Mrs Brown. Baillie Slorach and Mrs Slorach, Baillie Gunn and Mrs Gunn. Baillie Frank Cassells and Mrs Cassells. Treasurer P. E. Soutter. Dean of Guild Anderson and Mrs Anderson. Ex Baillie Cassells and Mrs Cassells, Councillor W Sneddon and Mrs Sneddon, Councillor J. M. Graham and Mrs Graham . . .

Death of Glasgow Journalist:

Mr David Howie, who was a well-known journalist, died at his residence, Glencairn, Strathaven, late on Sunday evening. Deceased was 74 years of age, and was born at Cupar - Fife. In 1869 he joined the reporting staff of the "Glasgow Herald" with which he continued his connection till 1906, when he retired. It was mainly through his exertions that a district of the Newspaper Press Fund was formed for the West of Scotland in February 1892, and he acted as chairman of the local committee for over fifteen years. At an early age of his journalistic career Mr Howie made a special study of military affairs, and for many years he attended the annual gathering of the National Rifle Association and similar bodies. In 1887 he wrote a history of the 1st Lanarkshire Volunteers, now the 5th Battalion Scottish Rifles.

School Board:

The usual monthly meeting was held on Tuesday, Dr. Mason, chairman of the Board, presided. It was decided, in order to avoid the risk of necessitating an increase in the Parish rate, to accept £50 net from the Parish Council as a contribution from the rates than the sum asked last year. The Visiting Committee's report on the evening classes was adopted. The Clerk submitted a report on the condition of Crosshill School and he was instructed to procure estimates for the necessary repairs. He also presented a report on the condition of Drumclog School buildings, and as the amount involved was considerably over £10 it was decided in this case also to take estimates. The Clerk submitted a letter from Michael McGovern's agent offering terms of settlement of the decree recently obtained against him, and he was instructed to accept these.

Issue: Saturday, 18 July, 1914.

Fair Week Attractions:

Monday, 18 yards quoiting handicap at Ward. "The Merry Makers" in the Public Park twice daily, dances in Public Hall every night, pleasure drives from some of the hiring establishments; the pictures each evening - for particulars see advertisements.

Thunderstorm:

A short sharp thunderstorm passed over the parish on Sunday between one and two o'clock p.m. In a short time the streets were like miniature rivers owing to the drains being unable to cope with the volume of water. There was a little flooding in the low lying part of Green Street and at Whitelaw Farm (Mr. Dykes) three cows were killed by the lightning.

Song writing:

Congratulations to Bro. James C. Stewart, chief templar of "Drumclog Lodge" L.O.G.T., on winning first prize in a song writing competition organised by "The Good Templar" the organ of the Grand Lodge of Scotland, L.O.G.T., and open to all comers. The competition consisted in writing a song having reference to the Temperance (Scotland) Bill and 1920 (the coming into full operation). Mr. Stewart's words are sung to the tune the "Marsellaise". A frequent contributor to our "Poets Corner" and to other magazines, Mr. Stewart is well known amongst lovers of the muse.

Unkempt Roads:

"Sir,

It is a great pity that the pleasant little town of Strathaven should be spoiled to a great extent by the roads leading into it in presenting such an unkempt and uncared for appearance. Surely the party responsible must be a direct descendant of "Rip Van Winkle". The grass and weeds on the roadsides, and bordering the footpaths are a perfect nuisance, especially on the road leading to the village of Chapelton. In wet weather you can't possibly go from the path to the roadway without getting your dress wet, unless you have a companion to hold the grass aside. Should the Parish Council not wish to rouse their superior from his peaceful rest, they might invite the stranger within their gates to a day or two's tidying up. a "Knut".

Issue: Saturday, 25th July, 1914.

Visitors get out of hand:

At the J. P. Court, Hamilton, on Monday, Andrew Kilon (40) iron turner, residing at Queenshill Street, Glasgow, was fined 15s, with the option of ten days in prison, for breach of the peace. Accused got the worse of drink on Thursday evening and was refused admission to his mother-in-law's house in Green Street, with the result that he created a disturbance. The same occurred again on Saturday, and at two a.m. on Sunday he became so noisy that he had to be taken in charge by the police. Two other cases are pending against Glasgow visitors for misbehaving during the week.

Golf Club:

Taking advantage of the large influx of golfing visitors this week, the committee decided to hold a Gala week, which has proved a great success. The prize-winners were as follows;-
Saturday (mixed foursomes competition) - 1st Miss Stewart and Mr Hamilton, 96 (less 14) - 82; 2nd, Miss V. Holland and Mr D. McLean, 101 (less 18.½ - 82.½. Monday (Gent's stroke competition) Mr R.D. Hamilton, 84 (less 10) - 74; and Rev. T. McRorie, 90 (less 16) 74. Tuesday (mixed foursome competitions) - Miss J. Bertram and Mr A. Hamilton, 48 (less 5) - 43; Miss M. Holland and Mr T.M. Weir 53 (less 10) - 43. Wednesday (clock golf competition) - 1. Mr J. Guthrie, 2. Mr D.C. Thomson, 3. Mr D. McLean. On Friday evening a pitching and putting competition proved an attraction; while on Saturday another mixed foursomes competition will complete a splendid golfing week.

Motoring Smash:

In Hamilton J.P. Court on Monday the sequel to the recent smashing of the lamp-post and gate pillar at the Strathaven Public Park was heard, when two young men were charged with having been drunk while in charge of the motor car which did the damage in the early morning hours of Thursday, 25th June. Both pleaded not guilty and a long trial ensued. The evidence of three Strathaven constables was to the effect that both men were drunk when the police arrived on the scene, and that there had been an alarming and serious smash. The men were staggering and unable to understand what was said. They were also smelling strongly of drink. For the defence, a complete denial of the charge was pled, and it was maintained that the glass screen of the car had got blurred by the rain and that the accident had occurred through this. It was also contended for the defence that the car was going at a moderate pace at the time and that the condition of the men as stated by the 3 constables was due to the severe shock and injury caused by the accident, and to the subsequent loss of blood. The car track for a period of 300 yards on the East Kilbride side of the lamp-post showed that the car was going straightly and properly before the collision. The Justices held the charge not proven, and the two accused were discharged from the bar. Mr. J. B. Ritchie, solicitor Hamilton and Mr. McFarlane Paterson, solicitor, Strathaven defended the accused.

The Fair Week:

Never probably in the history of Strathaven as a health and holiday resort had there been so many strangers within her gates as during the last week. From Thursday onward every train was packed, and the influx was so great on Friday and Saturday that one was inclined to wonder where all the people were going to be lodged. Saturday was only a moderately good day, but from Sunday onward the weather has been ideal, with the result that the visitors have been able to get out and about with the utmost freedom. The churches were well filled on Sunday, and the open-air meeting in the George Allan Park in the afternoon had a record attendance. On Monday those who did not make special programmes for themselves divided their attention between the "Merrymakers" in the Public Park, the gala day at Sandford, the quoiting tournament at the Ward, and walk to the shrine of good John Brown of Priestgill at Auchingilloch, organised and conducted by the Rev. James McRorie of the West United Free Church. On Tuesday the local Co-operative Society arranged a trip to Girvan and this was largely taken advantage of by the visitors. Picnic parties were to be found everywhere with the ever-popular Primrose Braes claiming the largest number. Each evening during the week, with the exception of Tuesday, there have been dances in the Public Hall, and these have been largely taken advantage of; whilst the local carriage and motor hirers have been taxed to their utmost to find accommodation for the large numbers anxious to take advantage of the pleasure drives arranged by them. Exceptional interest has been taken in the Castle and other ancient places in the neighbourhood and visitors are freely expressing their pleasure at the enterprise of the Parish Council in making excavations at the Castle and the Town Improvement Committee and the County Council for their operations throughout the town. With reference to the Castle, we have been in the way of hearing some of the visitors tell others "what the landlady said about the Castle," and we are inclined to think there has been a good deal of "pulling the long bow," or perhaps our own knowledge of the Castle's history is defective. Taken all in, the week has been a red letter one in the experience of many a city toiler, and we are confident they will return to office and workshop greatly the better of their sojourn in our ancient township.

Issue: Saturday, 8th August, 1914.

Grave European Crisis:

Since the Union of the Crowns no conflict in which this country has been engaged has stirred the masses of the people or touched them so closely and at so many points as the Titanic struggle upon which the Government has now embarked in the maintenance of British interests and the integrity of a small, but brave European State. The feeling that we are up against something serious began to manifest itself towards the end of last week when Germany was pressing both Russia and France for assurances. A great Continental War being feared, the notion that food supplies would become scarce and dear induced people to make an abnormal demand upon their grocer, with the inevitable result that the prices of such necessary commodities as sugar, flour etc., went steadily up. The tension during the week-end in Hamilton was intense. The probabilities of the situation were almost the sole topic of discussion. The news of Germany's declaration of war against Russia was received in the town early on Sunday morning and it spread like wild fire, afterwards receiving confirmation through special war editions of the Glasgow evening newspapers. These were bought up with avidity, and read with an eagerness that indicated the hold which the momentous march of events had on the public mind. References to the war and the dramatic breaking-up of European peace were made in most of the churches on Sabbath by the respective clergymen, and prayers for the maintenance of peace, as well as for guidance and wisdom to our rulers in the crisis which had so suddenly arisen ascended from every pulpit. Still more eventful was the news at the beginning of the week, but after having been accustomed to the astonishing aggressiveness which had marked the course of German diplomacy during these past few days, the public were not unprepared for the startling rupture which involved our country in a war with our most virile competitor in the field of commerce and the greatest world-power after our own. Never, it may be safely said, have the people of Hamilton of all classes shown such an interest in the newspapers as they did during the hours which witnessed the failure of diplomacy, the invasion of Belgian neutrality by the forces of the Kaiser, the ultimatum to Germany, its rejection and the consequent declaration of war. These events followed each other with amazing rapidity. There was, however, no excitement and no exhibition of the jingo spirit. It was all the other way. The feeling was that, through no fault of our own, we had been brought up against a set of circumstances from which there could be no turning back, but only a going forward with all the perils, and vicissitudes which that step involved. The prices of food-stuffs still went up. Grocers in the town were cleaned out of sugar and flour in some instances, and on Tuesday one large wholesale and retail firm closed its doors, being unable to cope with the demand, and a few other shops had to adopt a similar course. The rise in price of commodities is not due to any scarcity, but was wholly occasioned by the people themselves unnecessarily laying up a supply of provisions against a fancied evil day. The assurances that have since been given by the Government at its masterly and immediate way of maintaining our normal supplies have had their effect, producing a more settled feeling, and though prices are not likely to assume their ordinary level while the spectre of war stalks across the seas, the public are assured that the necessity for an abnormal increase is as yet quite unwarranted. The people will, therefore, do well and will be consulting the general interest by keeping to their ordinary supplies instead of selfishly overstocking and thereby creating scarcity which does not really exist. The gravity of the situation came more home to people when the mobilisation orders were issued for the immediate embodiment of the Naval and Army Reserve and the Territorials. Since that moment Hamilton has been like an armed camp. *"The call of the pibroch and the marching of men."* have been familiar sounds. From all parts of the country the Reserves of the H.L.I. and the Scottish Rifles arrived in Hamilton and made their way to the Barracks from which, during each evening this week, they have issued in the uniform of the regiment. And been drafted off in companies 200 and 300 to their respective stations. Crowds assembled in the vicinity of Hamilton (C.R) station and gave the Reserves a hearty send off

Drunk and Incapable:

Mary Conway or Flannery, vagrant, was fined 5s, or three days at Hamilton J.P.Court on Wednesday.

War Scare - Suspected German Spy:

A man of German appearance with motor car was stopped by police and questioned in Kirk Street on Thursday which caused rather a sensation at the time. However, things turned out to be all in order, and there is no occasion for alarm at Strathaven as yet.

Property Sales:

On Tuesday, in the Public Hall, the farm of North Carnduff, with a rental of £76 was sold at the reduced upset price of £1200. A tenement of houses, 17 Glassford Road, with a rental of £32, and a feu duty of £1.4.10d was unsuccessfully offered at £350. The Strathaven Auction Mart. Ltd., were auctioneers, and Messrs. J & J. Barrie, writers, agents in the sales.

The Burglary at Shalimar Villa:

At a pleading diet at Hamilton on Thursday, James Wallace, 13 Govan Street, Glasgow and John Small, 219 Commercial Road, Glasgow were charged with having on 1st July broken into Shalimar Villa, Crosshill, Strathaven and stolen a silver card case, a silver bangle, 9 silver coins, and 2/6d in money. They pled not guilty and were continued till 25th August for trial by jury.

10th Royal Scots Cyclist Corps:

A company of the above corps from East Linton, under command of Captain Mason, arrived in Strathaven on Wednesday evening. The company consisted of 50 rank and file, 5 sergeants and one lieutenant. Form of billeting requisitioning was served on the police about 6.30 p.m. the company arriving about 9 p.m. 27 were billeted with Mr. A. Taylor, Bridge Street and 30 with Mr. William Sommerville, Kirk Street. The company were en-route to Dundonald, Ayrshire.

Issue: Saturday, 15th August, 1914.

Open-Air Mission:

Mr. Hill, the well known evangelist conducts meetings tomorrow - See advert.

Public Hall as Hospital:

At a meeting of the directors of the Public Hall it was unanimously resolved to offer the Government the use of the hall for hospital or convalescence purposes.

A Quarrelsome Labourer:

At the J.P. Court, Hamilton, on Monday, Robert Wilson, labourer, Castle Street, was fined 15s, with the option of ten days in prison for assault and breach of peace on Saturday night. Accused had been in the Castle Bar, and had endeavoured to pick a quarrel with a man who was standing at the counter. Remonstrated with by the barmaid, he used abusive language to her and wound up by throwing the contents of his beer measure in her face.

Farm Fire:

About 3.30 o'clock on Monday afternoon fire was discovered to have broken out at Hareshawhead Farm (Messrs. Semple and Rankin's). The farm hands and neighbours made a determined attack on the fire with the apparatus at their disposal and separated the roof from that of the farm house which adjoins whilst a cyclist made for Bonnanhill from whence the police were notified. Within forty-five minutes of the call the Larkhall Detachment of the County Fire Brigade was on the scene and with a liberal supply of water from the Hareshaw Burn, got the outbreak completely under control. The damage to buildings, which are insured, amounted to about £40, and to hay, which was not insured, about £18.

Avondale War Relief Fund:

At a meeting in the Public Hall, Strathaven, on Thursday, held to consider the present position of affairs, it was agreed that every effort should be made to assist, and a large and representative committee was formed, with the Town Improvement Committee as a nucleus; Mr James Cameron, C.C., and Mr James Barrie, Cullenpark, as joint conveners; and Mr Alex Wilson as secretary and treasurer. Mr Cameron explained generally the object of the meeting, and reported as to the county meeting that day in Glasgow. Mr James Barrie detailed various methods by which everyone could help, emphasising the duty laid on all at home to assist those bearing the burden of our defence. Mr James Pollok (Overton) spoke in support of the training of all men, 17 to 50 years of age, and his views were unanimously endorsed. Strathaven is fortunate in having competent resident instructors, and Sergeant-Major W. O. Robert Jennings, who gave full details of the week volunteered his services which were cordially accepted. Representatives of the various churches were invited, and agreed to attend to the soup kitchen (so long carried on by the Rev. A.W. Donaldson), in co-operation with the School Board. As the best method of raising funds, and to avoid any overlapping, it was unanimously decided to make a house-to-house collection, in aid of national and local requirements as the committee might find advisable, any donations to a special fund to be applied as wished. - See advertisement.

Hamilton Ministers and the War:

Last Sabbath, spirited references to the war were made by the Rev. J. H. Deas in Hamilton Memorial U.F. church and the Rev. James Wallace in the Congregational Church. Mr Deas preached from the text *"If it be possible, as much as lieth in you, live peaceably with all men."* In the course of an eloquent and patriotic sermon, he stated that he had no hesitation about the righteousness of our going to war, and added that Sir Edward Grey, the Foreign Secretary, had exhausted the Apostolic precept which enjoined *"as much as lieth in you, live peaceably with all men."* The theme of Mr Wallace's discourse was *"The Higher Patriotism."* He emphasised the need, in a time of crisis like the present, of remembering our indebtedness to God; not to be boastful and proud, but *"Unto God be all the glory."* In the Parish Church on Sunday last intercessory services were held morning and evening. At both services the minister, the Rev. J. W. Wilson made reference to the present war. At the evening service Mr Wilson said:- *War is a terrible thing, even in the interests of righteousness and honour and self-sacrifice for fellow men. We differ from Ruskin when he says "All great nations learned their truth of word and strength of thought in war; that they were nourished in war and wasted by peace."* We think as we live in the meridian splendour of Christianity that we know *something better, and that is the peace and charity of Christ. The British people know the value of peace, and are absolutely opposed to the man whose supreme desire is for power and lawlessness. We never experienced a bad peace. O! the infinite pity that the peace of this land has been broken. The utmost was done by our peace-loving king and statesmen to avert war. But we have been thwarted. War has been thrust upon us. And now we are face to face with a conflict which for magnitude is unparalleled in the history of the world. It was almost an impossibility that Britain could stand aside. Justice and honour and the weaker nations and fidelity to our treaty obligations furnish adequate reason for Britain's interference. She never made a nobler stand. We still stand as in the days of our forefathers, for the principles of humanity, justice, loyalty and religion. We characterise the declinature of the German Emperor to take part in the peaceful conference of the Powers as an irrational judgment. And it is a matter for infinite regret that he proposed that Britain should agree that Germany should be allowed to march through Belgium to attack France, thus placing Belgium, Holland, Norway and Sweden open to her army and fleet. It was then that the British stepped in between the lawless spoiler and the weak and intimidated. "I shall protect Belgium by land and sea" and the other weak powers should necessity arise. So Britain became involved. God made us equal to our high trusts, our great responsibilities, and this tremendous task. Let us humble ourselves before him, and pray that our soldiers and sailors may be blessed with inspiration and faith and courage, and that a glorious victory may come to our fleet and army and peace be restored. "Peace hath her victories no less renowned that war."* The hymns at both services were most appropriate. The morning service was opened by the Psalm "God is our Refuge and our Strength," and was closed by the singing of the National Anthem. In the evening, special music was given by the choir. Rudyard Kipling's "Recessional Hymn" was rendered by four members of the choir - Miss Emily Hornal, Miss Susan Gray, Mr James Curr, and Mr William Curr. The choir made an excellent contribution to the service. Mr Taylor presided at the instrument.

Issue Saturday, 22nd August, 1914.

A Rare Avis:

A beautiful specimen of the kingfisher was seen on one of the tributaries of the Avon on Thursday, 20th inst. It is to be hoped that this rare visitation may remain.

Handy Boy Scouts:

Following an offer made to the Chief Constable of Lanarkshire, the local patrol of Boy Scouts have this week been employed to distribute to every house in Avondale and Stonehouse parishes and in the village of Sandford, war fund leaflets issued by the County Committee. The police bear testimony to the eager and efficient manner in which the boys have carried out their work.

War Relief Fund:

Attention is directed to the first list of subscriptions to this fund - amounting to £426.8s.8d - advertised on page 7. The committee are to be congratulated on the result, as well as on the splendid manner in which all their schemes have been organised. During the coming week collectors will be at work in the various districts throughout the parish, and it is hoped that everyone will do what they can to help, according to their means.

Red Cross Week

In response to an intimation read from the church pulpits, and published throughout the town, a large gathering of ladies took place in the Parish Church Hall on Tuesday, 16th inst., at 2.30 p.m. Mrs. Lee Dykes of East Overton, presided, and gave out a large quantity of wool and flannel, etc., to be converted into socks, bed jackets and night shirts for our troops in the field. So eager and hearty was the response to the intimation that the supplies had to be renewed, and in the evening at 7 p.m. quite as big a gathering again assembled, clamouring to be supplied with material. The committee of the local war relief fund at their meeting on Monday co-opted Mrs Lee Dykes, Miss Greenshields Leadbetter, Mrs Alan Watt, and Miss Jane Whyte Cochran as members of the executive.

Suspected Fire Raising:

On Tuesday of last week an outbreak of fire occurred about 3.30 o'clock in the afternoon at the farm of Hareshawhead, tenanted by Mr A. Rankin. A visitor at the farm, in the person of Mr Graham, schoolmaster, Motherwell, mounted his bicycle and riding to Bonnanhill, the residence of Mr Alex. Ross, writer, there summoned by telephone the County Fire Brigade from Larkhall, which, on arrival, was successful in confining the fire to the barn in which it had originated. The damage done, however, was considerable. There was no one working about the farm steading on the two following days, all the men being out at the shooting. On Friday morning, when the girl went out to bring in the cows, she discovered the hay shed to be on fire. Mr Graham again cycled to Bonnanhill and summoned the fire brigades from Lanark and Larkhall. They arrived within three quarters of an hour of the alarm being given. The fire spread from the hay shed to two byres, cheese house, boiler house and scullery. A large quantity of hay was destroyed, together with some valuable farm implements, and a pony trap. The loss to the farmer, unfortunately, is not covered by insurance. The dwelling-house was saved almost by a miracle, the morning being very calm. Had there been a breeze, the dwelling-house must have been also burned. Two detective officers have been making searching inquiries during the week into the occurrence which is suspected t be a case of fire raising.

Volunteer Company Raised:

In response to an invitation convened through our advertising columns, and by bills, a large number of men assembled in the Public Hall on Monday evening for the purpose of enrolling in a Volunteer Company to prepare drafts for the Territorials and train for home defence. Mr James Cameron, C.C., who presided, explained that there was no intention of interfering with Lord Kitchener's plans in the formation of this company; as a matter of fact they considered his Lordship's appeal as of first importance, and urged all men with the specified ages to join the regular army for a period of three years or during the duration of the war. Rev. John Muirhead, B.D., followed with a vigorous speech, in which he expressed the hope that the company would be successfully formed so that even at this late hour the men of Avondale might do something to put themselves in a state of preparedness to do their share of the nation's work. Sergeant-Major Jennings, W.O., and Mr T. Greenshields Leadbetter, J.P., having explained what provision would be made for the dependents of those joining the colours, enrolments were invited. Three volunteered for the front, and were attested in the Parish Council Offices, The remainder marched to the John Hastie Park, where four squads were formed under the instructorship of No.1 Squad, Col-Sergt. Hugh Ritchie; No.2 Squad, Sergt. James M. Bryson; No. 3 Squad, Sergt. David McKay; No.4 Squad, Corporal Robert Downie; No.5 Squad, Cadet John Wilson. Colour Sergt. Instructor J. Kennedy takes each of the five sections alternately in the Academy Hall for gymnastics. The first drill took place on Tuesday evening in the John Hastie Public Park, when the muster amounted to over one hundred - Sergeant-Major Jennings supervising the instruction given by the section commanders. On Wednesday evening the National Reservists of the district paraded. The Manager of the local Picture House has risen to the occasion, and intimates that National Reservists and Volunteers will be admitted to the pictures at half-price.

Floral and Horticultural Society:

As intimated in our advertising column, the annual fixture of this society, which was to have come off on Saturday next, has been cancelled on account of the war.

Soldier and Sailors Families Association:

The wives and dependants of soldiers and sailors should send in their names to the association of the above society, whose names will be found on the window bills in the district.

Shalimar Burglars Sentenced:

The final act of the burglary at Shalimar took place at the Sheriff Court, Hamilton, on Tuesday, before Hon. Sheriff Stodart, and a jury, when James Wallace and John Small, the men implicated, were, after a lengthy trial, sentenced to nine months imprisonment. It is reported that on leaving the prison van at the gates of Barlinnie Prison, Wallace slipped the handcuffs and made a dash for freedom. He managed to run about a hundred yards, when he was overtaken and recaptured by his escort.

Volunteers:

The Parish of Avondale Local Volunteer Force continues to grow, and the numbers in Strathaven have now been increased to close on 150. During the week drills took place in the John Hastie Public Park on Monday and Wednesday under the instructors, Sergt. Major Jennings, W.O. supervising, and on Friday evening the entire force had a Route March. On Tuesday the Sergt. Major enrolled a number of men in Glassford and on Thursday several more were added to the force at Gilmourton. Col. Sergt. Instructor T. Kennedy conducts gymnastic classes every evening in the Academy. Intending recruits should make application for enrolment at once as the force will soon be closed for the present.

National Farmers' Union of Scotland Evening:

A meeting of the local branch, which embraces Avondale, Stonehouse, and Glassford Parishes, was held in the Auction Mart on Tuesday afternoon to consider what steps should be taken in view of the shortage of men and horses for the gathering of the harvest. There was a good attendance. It was intimated that Mr Alex Wilson had offered to establish a free registry at the Parish Council office, where names could be received of farmers requiring help, and workers willing to assist at the harvest. The offer was cordially accepted, and the secretary was instructed to advertise the fact in the "Hamilton Advertiser" and by bill. Mr J. Montgomarie Pierson presided.

National Reserve:

The National Reservists of Avondale paraded in the Commongreen on Sunday under Sergt. Major Jennings W.O., district secretary. Fourteen files (28 men) turned out and the "boys of the old brigade" really presented a fine appearance. After being photographed, the reservists marched to the Public Hall where district orders were read by the Sergt. Major. He explained that a section of the National Reserve had already been called out, viz., men up to 42 years of age who had served in the line, and that the next lot to be called on would be all men under 42 years of age belonging to Class 1. It was intimated that Mr Howat, Gilmourton, a member of Class 111, had died that morning, and the members agreed to attend the funeral on Wednesday.

Picture House Benefit Night:

The enterprising manager of the Picture House, Mr Joseph Darby, gave a benefit night in the Picture House on Thursday in favour of the Avondale War Relief Fund. There was a large attendance, especially in the higher priced seats, and the audience had full value for their money in an exceptionally fine selection of films. The sum available to be handed over to the fund is quite substantial.

Obituary:

A well know figure in the parish has been removed by death in the person of Mr James Howat, Gilmourton, retired gamekeeper. A man of exceptionally pleasant temperament, he was widely known and much respected. In the social life of the Gilmourton district he has for many years played a prominent part, being an enthusiastic member of the carpet bowling club, the Mutual Improvement Association, and other societies besides always being in the forefront in political life as a hard worker for the Unionist cause. The funeral to Strathaven cemetery took place on Wednesday, and the cortege was headed by Pipe-Major Donald Matheson as it wended its way thither. The effect of the playing and the slow, measured step was most impressive. Mr Howat is survived by his widow and a grown up family, for whom much sympathy is felt in their loss.

Police Loss:

During the week Constable John Pirrie, who has been stationed here for one year and ten months, was transferred to Bellshill. Constable Pirrie was very popular with all classes of the community, and showed by his demeanour that he fully realised the correct relations he ought, as a police constable, to bear to all. In connection with the recent burglary at Shalimar he distinguished himself by arresting single-handed, the two men concerned, a by no means mean feat when it is recollected that one at least of the men was an old jail bird and well-known cracksman. The appreciation of the Chief Constable was shown by the fact being recorded in the "orders" and the constable commended. Whilst sorry to lose this promising young constable, we feel sure that the best wishes of the Strathaven public will go with him to his new sphere.

Children's Flower Show:

This annual event in connection with the Sabbath School of Avondale Parish Church took place in the Hall on Saturday. Section 1. Sweet peas is raised from the seeds distributed by the minister in that spring to all who signify their intention of competing. In all the sections a most creditable display was made, and with the addition of some fine vases of sweet peas from the Manse gardens, the hall presented a fine appearance. Rev. John Muirhead, B.D., who is well known as a skilful horticulturist, judged the classes and made awards as follows:- Section 1. Best vase of Sweet Peas not more than 10 spikes - Girls 1. Jeanie Kyle, Thomson Street, 2. Chrissie B . Knox. Parklea, 3. Rena Dempster, Thorntree Cottage, Best Vase of Sweet Peas not more than 10 spikes. Boys - 1. Robert Kyle, Sandknowe. Quite a number of visitors attended the exhibition during the course of the afternoon, and much interest was evinced in the efforts of the youngsters.

Avondale War Relief Fund:

A meeting of committee was held in the Lesser Hall, Kirk Street, on Wednesday night - Mr James Cameron, C.C. in the chair. A letter from the Middle Ward District Committee was read intimating that a committee had been constituted to undertake the administration of the National Relief Fund in their district, and suggesting that a local committee should be formed for Avondale. It was unanimously agreed that the existing committee should be merged into a General Committee with representatives of all classes added. The following were appointed as an Executive Committee:- Mrs

Lee Dykes, Mrs Watt, Mrs Lusk, Mrs Cameron, Miss Dougan, Mr James Cameron (convener), Mr James Barrie (vice convener), Dr. Mason, Messrs. Wm. Dykes, R.B. Galloway, John Bertram, Wm. Watson, Wm. Ruthven, John Wiseman, John Campbell, Patrick Wynn, and Alex. Wilson (secretary and treasurer) The sum of £50 was unanimously voted to the Belgian Relief Fund. Votes of thanks were cordially awarded to Mr Cameron (chairman) and Mr Wilson (secretary) for their services.

The Crosshill Villa Burglary:

In Hamilton Sheriff Court on Tuesday - before Hon. Sheriff Stodart and a jury - the trial took place of James Wallace, merchant, 13 Govan Street, Glasgow, and John Small, clerk, 219 Commercial Road, Glasgow, on a charge of being concerned in the recent burglary at Crosshill, Strathaven. The complaint which was at the instance of the Lord Advocate bore that on the 1st of July last, the accused had broken into the dwelling house known as "Shalimar" Villa at Crosshill, occupied by Henry Hind Hamilton, merchant, and stole therefrom a silver card-case, a silver bangle with nine coins attached thereto, and 2/6d of money. For the prosecution, thirteen witnesses were summoned. These included the aforesaid Henry H. Hamilton, Mary Jackson Hamilton (daughter), Margaret Jackson or Hamilton (wife), Mrs. Watson or Hamilton, Crosshill Avenue; Catherine Brown or Coats and John Coats, Crosshill Dairy; Robert Kirkwood (boy) 76 East Thornlie Street, Wishaw; Gavin Hyslop (13) Gavinbank, Crosshill; James Ballantyne (boy) Letham Road; Robert Semple, joiner, 5 Commercial Road, Strathaven; Thos. Sommerville, joiner, 22 Southend, Strathaven; Constables John Pirie and Alexander Clark. The examination of these witnesses occupied fully three hours. The case for the Crown was conducted by Mr William Thomson, Procurator- Fiscal, while Mr George McLaughlin, writer, Hamilton appeared for the defence. The evidence for the Crown went to show that the 1st July was a holiday in Strathaven and that the occupants of Shalimar Villa had gone away for the day. In the early afternoon, a neighbour woman, while upstairs in a room which overlooked Shalimar Villa, saw two men enter that villa by the back door. Knowing that the occupants were on holiday, she gave the alarm, and along with another woman and some boys proceeded to Shalimar Villa from which a noise upstairs was heard. Just as the women proceeded round to the back of the house, two men came hurriedly out by the back door, and they made off through the croquet green climbing a fence into a park, thence to Townhead Street. One of the men was carrying an overcoat and the other an umbrella. It was afterwards found that the back door lock of Shalimar Villa had been tampered with, while a chair was found tilted up against the inside of the front door to prevent it being opened from the outside. The two front bedrooms were in disorder, drawers having been ransacked. Witnesses also spoke to being shown later on two men at the Police Office whom they identified as the two men they had seen coming out of the villa. The two accused in the dock were, they said, the two men they identified at the Police Office. The evidence of the boys went to show that while one of them made off to inform the police, others went over the fence after the two men through the park. In Townhead Street, two constables on bicycles were told by the boys of what had occurred at the villa, and the officers made off in opposite directions. Two men were afterwards seen in a hayfield on the other side of the railway as if making for the station. They were taken into custody by the police and were identified by the boys as the men who had ran out of Shalimar Villa. An umbrella was also found near the place where the men were seen standing. The evidence of the constables detailed the manner in which the accused were arrested, and their subsequent identification by witnesses. No witnesses were examined for the defence, but Mr McLaughlin, in addressing the jury on behalf of the accused, strongly urged that this was a case of mistaken identity, and that the two accused were not the two men who were seen to come out of Shalimar Villa on the date libelled. He reminded the jury that if there was raised in their minds the least shadow of a doubt, then the accused were entitled to the benefit of it. The jury then retired to consider their verdict. They were only absent for a few minutes, when they returned with a unanimous verdict of guilty against both accused. The Procurator-Fiscal, at this stage, intimated a previous conviction against each of the accused for theft by housebreaking. Mr. McLaughlin reminded the Court that the convictions were fully four years old, and that in the case of Small he had been dismissed by the High Court with an admonition. He further urged for a lenient sentence being imposed, remarking that he believed it was the firm intention of the accused, at this period of national crisis, to join the colours. The Sheriff said, taking all the circumstances into account, he could not impose a lesser sentence that that of nine months' imprisonment each.

Golf Club:

Gentleman's Competition for Bronze Medal - Today Ladies' Competition on Wednesday 9th. Whole of Entry Money for War Relief Fund. W.H. Secy.

Issue: Saturday, 5th September, 1914.

United Prayer Meeting:

Under the auspices of the churches of the town, a prayer meeting of intercession in connection with the war was held in the hall of the West UF Church on Thursday evening and was largely attended.

Accident:

A serious accident occurred to a boy named Thos. Smith, about 9 years of age in Green Street, on Tuesday. He had been running to take a ride on the shaft which connects the threshing mill with the engine of Gray & Paterson's turn-out when he slipped on a banana skin and fell. A wheel of the mill passed over his face inflicting fearful injuries. This little chap was picked up and carried to Dr. Mason's dispensary where he was attended to and afterwards removed to the Royal Infirmary, Glasgow.

Strathaven:

Wanted: Board or rooms in Strathaven or vicinity, for Patient about to leave Sanatorium. Apply Bryson, Printer.

Mr. Thomas Rankin, L.D.S., Dental Surgeon, 66 Cadzow Street, Hamilton visits Strathaven every Tuesday, from two p.m. till eight p.m. Consulting Rooms - 14 Commongreen (Mrs. Robinson's).

Issue: Saturday, 12th September, 1914.

National Relief Fund:

Competitions for bronze medals presented by "Golf Illustrated" were held at the Golf Course on Saturday 5th inst, and Wednesday 9th inst. The medal for the best scratch score was won by D. McLean, who returned a card of 83. Andrew Hamilton (14) won the first-class medal with a score of 72, and Alan Broom (18) won the second-class with a net score of 79. In the Ladies' Section, the medal was won by Miss Cathie Wilson. As a result of the competition the sum of

£4.10s.6d has been handed over to Mr Alexander Wilson, local treasurer, Prince of Wales Fund.

Disturbing the Harvesters:

Thomas Scott, farm servant, High Cauldcoats, was at the J.P. Court, Hamilton, on Monday, charged with breach of the peace by disturbing Wm. Bryson and family in harvest field on Saturday last. Complaints were received on previous days, and on date in question a constable in plain clothes assisted at the harvest and apprehended the accused on renewing this disturbance. He was fined 15s or ten days in prison - Mary McLeary or Shields (44) of no fixed residence, was at the same Court fined 15s or ten days for breach of the peace on Saturday night.

Soup Kitchen:

At a meeting of the ministers of the town it was unanimously agreed to carry on this beneficent institution so long conducted under the able management of Mr Donaldson, minister emeritus of the East United Free Church. Mr Donaldson was present, and agreed to act as convener of the committee. Mr John Torrance, writer, has kindly undertaken the work of secretary and treasurer, and will be pleased to receive subscriptions from all who were in the habit of helping Mr Donaldson in this work and of any others who may be inclined to assist. It is earnestly hoped that the inhabitants, with their accustomed liberality, will support this institution under its new management, as the coming winter may be a very trying one.

Route March:

The local volunteer company which has now increased in number to 150, together with the Boy Scouts, had a route march on Friday evening last. Assembling in the John Hastie Park, the volunteers were put through a few movements by Sergt. Major Jennings after which they marched to Glassford. Here a halt was called in the square opposite the Public Hall, and addresses were delivered by the Sergt. Major and Rev. John Muirhead, B.D. (who is a member of the company) calling on the young men of Glassford to join Lord Kitchener's Army, and those who were too old for the front to form a volunteer company. The march was then resumed, the men returning via the Glassford Station Road and Whiteshawgate. The splendid appearance of the company was freely commented on. Music for the march was provided by Pipe Major Donald Matheson, the Duke of Hamilton's piper, and the young Marquis of Douglas and Clydesdale accompanied the march all the way.

Issue: Saturday, 19th September, 1914.

Temperance Lecture:

On Wednesday, 16th September, Mr Crosbie of the Scottish Band of Hope, gave an interesting and instructive temperance lecture to the senior scholars of the Academy. The subject was "The Dangers of Alcohol." The lesson was listened to attentively by the scholars and was evidently much enjoyed.

Police Promotion:

The many friends of Mr Matthew McCulloch will learn with pleasure of his promotion to the rank of superintendent in the Lanarkshire Constabulary. It will be recollected that Mr McCulloch was senior constable at Strathaven during that trying time when the Glengavel Waterworks were in process of construction when he handled the navvies with great tact. His services were rewarded by his promotion to Baillieston as sergeant and will, we understand, be in charge of the Lower Ward of Lanarkshire.

School Board:

A special meeting was held on Tuesday - Dr. Mason, Chairman of the Board, presided. Miss White, Larkhall, was appointed to the vacancy in the dressmaking class in the evening school. A letter was submitted from Sergeant Kennedy intimating that he had been called up to re-join the colours and had been posted as Musketry Instructor in Lord Kitchener's Army. It was decided to keep his appointment open for him and to advertise for someone to take charge of the janitor and School Board Officer during Sergt. Kennedy's absence. Mr Millar, headmaster of the Academy, intimated that the drill instruction could be undertaken meantime by the staff.

Comforts for the Territorials:

Sir, - I have received the following letter from the Chairman of the Lanarkshire Territorial Force Association, and I have willingly agreed to act. The comforts we are asked to provide for our soldiers are socks, shirts, knitted cholera belts, mittens, mufflers, and wristlets. They should all be grey or natural coloured wool, and any things that are sent to me will be gratefully received and forwarded to the proper quarters. May I at the same time avail myself of your valuable columns to express my sincere thanks to all those who have so willing worked for me for the Red Cross. - Yours faithfully,

May Greenshields Leadbetter

Stobieside, Drumclog, Sept. 16, 1914.

Issue: Saturday, 26th September, 1914.

Baptismal Ceremony at Dungavel:

On Tuesday last, the 15th September, the infant daughter of the Duke and Duchess of Hamilton was baptised in the private chapel at Dungavel in the presence of a large gathering of friends and tenantry. The name given is Mairi Nina, after her Majesty the Queen and the Duchess - Mairi being the Gaelic form of Mary. The service was conducted by the Rev. John Muirhead, B.D., minister of Avendale, and after the benediction the National Anthem was sung. At the conclusion of the ceremony the Duke and Duchess entertained the company in the billiard room, and there also were to be seen some beautiful presents bestowed upon Lady Mairi, the most beautiful being that of Queen Mary to her godchild - a lovely sapphire pendant. The Rev. Mr Muirhead proposed the health of the Duke and Duchess of Hamilton and Lady Mairi. It was, he said, a great joy and pleasure to them all to see the Duke and Duchess and family going out and in amongst them and taking such an active and foremost part in every good work. He thanked Their Graces for their kindness in inviting them to be present on that interesting occasion, and said that they were all proud of them and of their splendid family. Three hearty cheers were given for the Duke and Duchess and family, and the proceedings ended with the singing of "Auld Lang Syne."

Bowling Club:

The directors of this club have arranged for a special game this afternoon on behalf of the War Fund, when it is to be hoped there will be a large turnout of members and friends in support of this momentous occasion.

Mutual Improvement Association:

At a recent meeting of the Board of Management the question of having the usual weekly lectures during the ensuing winter was brought up, and after consideration it was unanimously agreed to carry on the work of the Association as in former years. The syllabus for the session has now been prepared, and it will be found that the lectures embrace a wide and varied range of subjects of interest to everyone. The opening lecture will take place on Monday week when Sheriff Hay Shennan will speak on "Law and Lawyers." A collection in silver was taken on behalf of the War Fund.

Avondale War Relief Fund Committee:

A meeting of the General Committee was held in the Lesser Public Hall on Monday evening - Mr James Cameron, C.C., in the chair. A very generous response having been made by the public to the appeal for funds, it was unanimously agreed to send £500 to the County Relief Fund and also a further sum of £60 making £110 to the Belgian Relief Fund. It was agreed to print in October a full list of subscriptions with a roll of honour containing the names of all in the district in service, and members of committee undertook to assist in making the roll as complete as possible. A Belgian Flag Day was arranged for Saturday, 3rd October, details being remitted to the lady members of the executive. A meeting of ladies willing to help is to be held on Monday evening. - See advert.

Ordination Service:

The Rev. James Charles Conn, only son of the late Mr Thomas Conn was ordained to the church and parish of Barrhead on Friday 189th inst., by the Presbytery of Paisley. The ordination took place in the Parish Church in the afternoon. The Rev. Robert Aitken, B.D., of St. George's, Paisley, preached and presided, and ordained the new minister; and the Rev. Arch. Halliday, of St. Andrew's Johnstone, delivered the charge to the minister and to the congregation. The church was crowded in every part, and there was a large turnout of the local clergy. A congregational social meeting was held in the evening in the Kirk to welcome the new minister. There were 1000 present. The Rev. Thomas Cook, M.A., of Levern, the moderator during the vacancy, presided, and addresses were given by the Rev. Dr. Smith of Partick, the Rev. J. Muirhead, B.D., of Avendale, and others. The new minister was presented with very handsome pulpit robes, and gratefully acknowledged the gifts. Throughout the evening a splendid programme was contributed by the choir and friends.

Issue: Saturday, 3 October, 1914.

Belgian Flag Day:

Today the ladies of the town will be collecting for the Belgian Relief Fund in the town whilst the Boy Scouts will visit the farms and outlying districts. Each distributor will receive a flag. It is hoped the people of Avondale will rise to the occasion with their usual generosity.

Local Soldier Wounded:

News has been received here with regret that Lieut. J.F.R. Gebbie of the Regiment South Lancashire, son of Mr. James Gebbie of Netherfield has been severely wounded on the 19th ult., and as a result has had his leg amputated. The latest report is that he is now doing well. Private Wright of the Seaforth Highlanders has also had his leg amputated and has also received nasty wounds to the hand and the chest.

Accident:

On Wednesday afternoon a boy named William Craig, residing in Castle Street, was cycling down Kirk Street and lost control of the machine at the cross. Unable to stop either to left or right he dashed into the window of Messrs. R & J. Orr's, Bakers, and sustained nasty cuts on the face and hands besides being rendered unconscious - On Thursday evening, a lad named John Stewart had his arm broken whilst gathering branches from trees at the Braes.

War Fund:

The first of a series of weekly collections on behalf of the War Fund was made in the Academy on Wednesday morning when the scholars contributed the sum of £2.7s. Like teachers in other parts of Scotland, the Academy staff are giving a certain percentage of salary each month to the same fund.

National Reserve Parade:

A parade of National Reservists of Avondale and Glassford Parishes will take place in the John Hastie Public Park tomorrow at three pm for inspection by Colonel James Stevenson, CB., ADC. The members of the Local Volunteer Force will parade at same place and time.

Horticultural Society:

The annual general meeting of this society was held in the Public Hall on Monday evening. Mr. A. Hamilton presiding. The treasurer submitted the financial statement for the year, which showed a balance on the debit side, and was considered very satisfactory. The office-bearers were re-elected as follows:- Hon, president, Mr. A McIntosh; vice-president, Mr. Robt. Leggate, jun.; treasurer, Mr. Thomson; secretary, Mr Wm. Cranston, Angle Street; assistant secretary, Mr Hamilton; with a large General Committee the convener being Mr Matthew Steele. B - was altered to allow of beetroot, carrots and parsnip being tabled without shaws. The list was revised and alterations were made in to a few of the classes. It was agreed that a class for six collarette dahlias. The classes were deleted from the schedule. - unanimously agreed to give a donation from the funds to the local War Fund. The prize money was then paid over to the successful competitors.

B.P. Boy Scouts:

The chairman of the School Board, Mr R. J. Naismith, J.P., succeeded in inaugurating the Boy Scout movement in the village and already 40 boys have joined. The boys are in the meantime being drilled by Scoutmaster Paton, Larkhall, a local official has been appointed. The boys have all taken the Scouts' pledge - That they promise to do his duty to God and the King. . . . .the Scouts' law, viz, a Scout's honour is to be trusted, is loyal, courteous, kind to all, a friend to all, and a brother to every Scout: smiles and whistles under all stances; clean in thought, word, and deed. It is proposed to have a church parade at a later date, when patrols in adjoining towns will take part. Saturday afternoon excursions are being arranged and the first will take place this afternoon. It is interesting to note that of the former Boy Scouts trained by Scout Paton all have received promotion in the Army. Though not intended to act as recruits for the Army, it forms a good training for any sphere in life which a boy may undertake. Mr. Alex. Anderson, Inspector, has agreed to act as president.

Issue: Saturday, 10th October, 1914.

Prize Station:

In the prize-list for best kept station on the Caledonian Railway the local station comes in second and earns £4 prize money. We congratulate Mr. Thorburn and his staff on having gone one better than last year, when the position was third. Owing to the tremendous stretch of bare rock at the station it is by no means an easy one to decorate.

Result of Belgian Flag Day:

The committee in charge of Saturday's effort are to be congratulated on the splendid result viz; the raising of £35.4s.6d. the ladies who were in charge of the town pursued their collecting with great enthusiasm. Not content to wait for customers on the street they routed them out of their houses to purchase the flags. The cyclist members of the Boy Scouts undertook the country districts and it is safe to say left few farms untouched. Thanks are also due to Mr. William Tennent, draper who presented each collector with an official badge free of charge. The amount collected which has been forwarded without deductions to the Central Fund represents 4d per head of the population in the area in which it was collected.

Lieut. Gebbie Dies of Wounds:

Information was received on Tuesday that Lieutenant James F.R. Gebbie, 2nd Battalion South Lancs Regiment who was reported in these columns last Saturday as having been wounded in the Battle of the Aisne had died on Sunday. Lieutenant Gebbie's wound was a severe one on the leg which necessitated its amputation in St. Nazaire's Hospital, near Nantes. After the operation the patient's condition was considered quite favourable, but he succumbed to his injuries on Sunday. Having studied away from Strathaven and passed into Sandhurst and thence to his regiment, Lt. Gebbie was not at all well known here but those who did know him looked upon him as a young man of considerable promise. He was 26 years of age and unmarried.

Issue: Saturday, 17th October, 1914.

War Lecture:

Attention is drawn to a lecture to be delivered on Monday first by a well-known native of the town Rev. W.M. Rankin, B.D. on his experience in Germany after the declaration of war - see advert.

Young Women's Christian Association:

At the opening meeting of the YWCA Mrs Dey, president presented the prizes given by the Home Bible Study Department to the members who had sent in replies to questions on the Book of Exodus. The names of the prize-winners are: Misses Mary Taylor, Maggie Taylor, Nellie Wiseman, Jeanie Reid, Barrie T. G. Thomson and Nettie Millar. The Association made a good start with a capital attendance.

Assault and Robbery:

On a Friday night about six weeks ago a Strathaven man named William Laidlaw, residing at Flemington missed the last train in Glasgow and was returning by Duke Street to spend the night with some friends when he was attacked by a band of young men and robbed of a watch and albert and 8s.10d in money. The sequel took place at the Sheriff Court, Glasgow, on Wednesday, when after trial by jury sentences varying from three to nine months imprisonment were passed on five of the prisoners and three were sent to the Borstal Institute for 3 years.

Strathaven Soldier Killed:

We regret to have to announce that Pte. Joseph Brownlie, 1st Battalion Cameron Highlanders was killed in action on Tuesday, 6th October. Further than the War Office letter to his mother Ms. Adam Brownlie, Ballgreen, there are no particulars of how the young man met his death. Pte. Brownlie was one of the regimental maxim gun team.

Fatal Accident at Boag Farm:

A sad accident resulting in the death of a young man named Alexander Welsh, aged 21, ploughman occurred at the Boag Farm (Mr. James Stobie's) on Tuesday. Welsh had been instructed to proceed to an outlying part of the farm to assist another man at draining and he took with him a miniature rifle for the purpose of having a shot at some wild duck in a pond by the way. Arrived at the place where draining was being carried out, he proceeded to show his companion how to drill. Bringing the rifle to the position "order arms" in which the butt rests on the ground he struck the butt on ground rather forcibly and the rifle went off. The ball passed through the lad's right eye and into his brain. A mounted messenger rode into the town for medical assistance and Dr. William Mason motored out. He was unable to do anything, however, and the lad died within an hour.

Issue: Saturday, 24th October, 1914.

Prisoner of War:

The many friends of Sgt. Peter Watson, Gordon Highlanders will be glad to learn that the uncertainty which had been felt to his fate has now been dispelled by the receipt of a letter stating that he is a prisoner in Germany. In the course of his letter, Peter says he is in perfect health. He and his fellow prisoners are not indulged in luxuries but they get plenty to eat and are well treated by their captors.

Benefit Concert:

We would draw special attention to the concert advertised in this issue to be held on Thursday first in aid of the Belgian Relief Fund. The organisers - Messrs. Guthrie and M.G. Hamilton - who rank high in the musical world, have seen to it that nothing but the best of fare is to be provided for the evening's entertainment. The Boy Scouts are also to have a hand in the programme. The concert is under the direct patronage of the Duke and Duchess of Hamilton.

Strathaven Soldier Killed:

We regret to announce the death of another Strathaven soldier viz; Pte. William Comar a reservist of the Camerons in action at the Battle of the Aisne on 16th September. He and Pte. Joseph Brownlie whose death was reported on Saturday last left together and agreed to "stick together" throughout the campaign. In civil life Pte. Comar was interested in temperance work in competition with the I.O.B and had charge of the juvenile tent. He gave useful instruction to the Scouts some time ago in signalling. Comar leaves a widow and a little girl, three years old, for whom much sympathy is felt.

Issue: Saturday, 31st October, 1914.

Off to the Front:

Mr. Robert A. Fleming who at the outbreak of the war enlisted in the Army Pay Corps left for the front on Monday. Previous to leaving he was presented with two pipes, a tobacco pouch, 1lb of tobacco and silver match box by the staff of the Record Office, No. 2 District, Hamilton where he has been stationed since joining.

Issue: Saturday, 7th November, 1914.

The "Belgian" Concert:

We are pleased to announced that as a result of the concert on Thursday evening Messrs. Guthrie and Hamilton have been able to hand over £16.17s to the Belgian Relief Fund.

New Photographs:

We have just received a new volume of photographs of Strathaven and Avondale in the shape of a postcard album recently published by Mr. A. Morton, Stationer. The views are all up-to-date and excellent in reproduction and are certain to cheer the hearts of natives at home and abroad. The album is unique in the get-up and possesses a counterfoil with a miniature picture of each photograph. It will make an appropriate xmas gift for posting to friends and the price is acceptable - ninepence.

Belgians in Strathaven:

There are now in all 21 refugees comfortably accommodated in Strathaven in five different houses, all of which, with several other houses were offered fully equipped free of rent. Several additional promises of weekly payments have been received, but more money is still required. The committee are now making a systematic canvas for contributions, and they trust that those interested will kindly come forward spontaneously with their offerings. Single payments of from £1 to £10 have also been received, the latter sum having been contributed by a Glasgow lady who hopes to be able to give another payment after Xmas. The committee gratefully acknowledge receipt of £10 from the Vale of Avon Amateur Athletic Club (per Mr David Hilston), of £16.17s. from Misses Guthrie and Hamilton, being one-half of the proceeds of the recent concert; £5 from the Strathaven Auction Mart., Ld., collection by Hallowe'en parties of boys, 34s, and of girls, 9s; and collection by Academy scholars, £2.4s. Three farmers are supplying each of the five houses with a quantity of potatoes. Each family of refugees is being looked after by two lady members of the committee. The committee also gratefully acknowledge many gifts of clothing. They have meantime put the other furnished houses available at the disposal of the Glasgow Corporation, subject to the approval of the committee. The committee would like to be informed of any farm work which could be had near the town. The head of one of the families has obtained temporary employment as a joiner, and two girls of another family are employed in Messrs. Elder & Watson's factory. In neither case is local labour being displaced. Two children are attending school. The women are to be supplied with material to work at home for Belgian wounded. Dr. Sarolea stated at a public meeting held in Musselburgh on Tuesday evening that while thousands of Belgians were already in this country, soon tens of thousands would be arriving. It is to be hoped therefore that the public will put the committee in funds for utilising more of the furnished houses which have been offered.

Issue: Saturday, 14th November, 1914.

Canadian Highlanders

During last week three Strathaven lads who have come to the country with the Canadian Highlanders paid a visit to their homes. The lads names are as follows:- Archibald Brownlie, son of Mr. Robt Brownlie, flesher, North Street, Robert Coats, son of Mr. Coats, Crosshill Farm and Alex Walker, son of Mr. Alex Walker, Todshill. All were looking fit and were full of enthusiasm and anxiety to get to the front.

Issue: Saturday. 28 November, 1914

Academy Collections for War Relief Funds:

Each Wednesday after devotional exercises a collection is taken from scholars on behalf of War Relief Funds. For nine weeks ended 15th inst., the sum raised in this way amounted to £15.13.9d.

Ambulance Class:

The class conducted annually by Dr. William Mason in connection with the local Caledonian Railway Staff has been resumed for the season. The meetings take place in the waiting room at the Central Station on Sunday afternoons and any young men who care to acquire useful first-aid knowledge are cordially invited to attend - For particulars see advert.

Kinderspiel:

The inauguration meeting in connection with the kinderspeil "Goldilocks and the Three Bears" which is to be produced in aid of the War Fund took place in the Lesser Public Hall on Wednesday evening. The turnout of children was most gratifying and the instructors are satisfied they have some good material to work on in connection with the production. The youngsters meet again on Wednesday.

For the Front:

Pte. Gavin Fleming of the Royal Army Medical Corps had a run home on Friday prior to leaving for the front. On Saturday evening he had a send-off by the Scouts of which, prior to joining the army, he was assistant Scoutmaster. Pte. Jack Riddell of the same corps left Aldershot for the front last week but did not have the privilege of leave as his section was sent off in a hurry. Pte. George Strachan remains at Aldershot meantime. All three lads got their preliminary instructions in ambulance work in the Boy Scouts.

Mutual Improvement Association:

There was a good attendance of members and friends on Monday evening to hear the Rev. C.W. Inglis Wardrop of Hamilton deliver a lecture on Shakespeare's "As You Like It". Mr. Wardrop said it was impossible for one to criticise anything written by such a master hand as Shakespeare, but he would endeavour to show what he considered to be the idea the great poet wished to convey when he wrote this play. This the reverend gentleman did in a most instructive and entertaining manner giving copious extracts from the play to illustrate his remarks.

East UF Church:

As already announced in our columns, the Rev. Matthew Urie Baird, M.A., assistant minister in North Woodside Church, Glasgow, is to be ordained and inducted to the pastorals of the East UF Church on Tuesday afternoon the 15th December. An Induction Social will be held the same evening at which, among others, the Rev. W. Forrest of Renfield Street Church, one of Glasgow's most attractive preachers to young men and women will take part. On the following Sunday special services will be held when the minister elect will be introduced to the congregation by the Rev. J. Sommerville Smith, Glasgow. As the Rev. A.W. Donaldson, B.A., minister emeritus only withdrew from active duty on the 30th June the congregation is to be congratulated on making such a speedy and harmonious settlement.

Soup Kitchen:

As reported in this column some time ago, a committee consisting of all the local clergymen with Mr. John Torrance as secretary has been formed to continue this work which has been carried on under the management of the Rev. Mr. Donaldson for so many years. The Soup Kitchen will this winter be conducted in the Great Templar Hall instead of the Mission Hall as formerly and commences on Monday first. The committee are deeply conscious of the many calls at present being made on the generosity of the public but they trust that the claims of this deserving institution will not be forgotten and that they will receive sufficient support to enable the work to be carried on in its present voluntary basis. Contributions either in cash or in the form of potatoes, vegetables etc., will be gladly acknowledged if intimated to any member of committee.

Another War Victim:

We regret to have to record the death of Pte. Gilbert McKinnon McArthur, 1st Btn Cameron Highlanders whose home address is in Castle Street. Pte. McKinnon rejoined the Cameronians on mobilisation and was almost immediately sent to the front. Until three weeks ago he was . . . and then he was wounded in the head and neck by shell. Removed to a London Hospital he was twice operated on and was supposed to be doing well. On Thursday, however, his wife received a summons by telegram to go and see him and shortly after her arrival he died. While lying in hospital, Pte. McArthur got intimation that he was winner of a second prize in a trench digging competition and his informant Captain Renwick wrote *"the best trenches have been shown to many soldiers of the Eastern Command who are shortly going to the front."* The deceased soldier was in the employment of Mr. R. W. Hamilton, Contractor, Waterside Street. He leaves a widow and two young children.

Strathaven Work Party:

The War Relief Committee and Mrs. Lee Dykes desire to thank very heartily all those ladies who have so generously contributed money and comforts for the benefit of our soldiers and sailors and Red Cross. Since the outbreak of the war the Work Party have met every Tuesday afternoon and evening, and as a result Mrs Lee Dykes has received in all 1185 articles exclusive of tobacco and cigarettes. These ladies have worked with the utmost zeal and enthusiasm and, as the demand for warm garments is still urgent and continuous, Mrs. Lee Dykes feels sure she can rely on having all the support required and she can always supply material to any who are willing to help every Tuesday afternoon and evening at the Parish Church Hall. The articles already supplied have been despatched to Her Majesty the Queen; to Hamilton Palace (450); Lady French (79); 6th Btn. Scottish Rifles (172); and to many others. Altogether 1200 articles sent.

Issue: Saturday, 12th December, 1914.

Boys and Girls Religious Society:

The annual business meeting of above was held in the Union Hall on Friday evening of last week when the financial statement showed a deficiency of £3. The number of young on the role was reported at 320 attending Sabbath morning worship and Sunshine Mission. Sabbath School workers on role 40. Mrs. Foulds has accepted presidentship in room of Mrs. T.F. Wilson resigned. Votes of thanks were awarded all round and a Christmas message was directed to be sent to the several workers who had joined the army.

Mutual Improvement Association:

"Toward Utopia" was the subject of a most interesting and instructive lecture delivered by Mr. John Semple of Lanark on Monday evening. There was a good attendance presided over by Mr. J. McFarlane Paterson. The subject, although a very comprehensive one, was treated in a very able manner by Mr. Semple who quoted many well known authors in support of his claim, that although our advancement seemed at times to be very slow, still, without doubt; it was sure and would ultimately lead to this desirable end. The lecture was freely criticised by several members present.

Issue: Saturday, 19th December, 1914.

Gilmourton School:

The pupils of Gilmourton School collected £3.10s to Princess Mary's fund for Her Royal Highness's Sailors' and Soldiers' Christmas Fund.

Christmas Concert:

Attendance is drawn to the advertisements column where particulars will be found of the annual Christmas Concert on behalf of the local Belgian Fund to be held on Monday, 21 December.

Princess Mary's Fund:

It is gratifying to report that the children attending Gilmourton School have been successful in collecting the sum of £3.10s towards Princess Mary's Soldiers' and Sailors' Christmas Fund. This will help in a little way to make the 'Tommies and 'Jacks' having a jolly Christmas.

Avondale War Relief Fund:

At a meeting of the Executive it was unanimously agreed to send a Christmas Box to all those on service from Avondale. About 130 substantial boxes have been despatched and fully 100 acknowledgements already received. Some extracts are annexed:- *"Thanks it was a splendid parcel - JH." "Everything comes in so useful here - ND." "Many thanks a lot of the chaps here wish they had been Strathaven men - WF." "It was very nice, I thought an awful lot of it. All my chums were round about me when I got the box and when they saw the shortbread and the cigarettes didn't they half shout - GB." "Sincere thanks for the magnificent box, my tent mates think there is nothing to beat Strathaven shortbread. All honour to Strathaven for leading the way - HW." "I consider it a welcome gift and it gives a youth more heart when he knows those at home remember him - WM." "Kindly thank the committee. The woollen articles are very handy. We are all looking forward for a trip to Berlin - JG." "I would like to thank the committee as everything will come in very useful and handy - AB." "I have no words to express my appreciation of the kindness of Stra'ven people - MH." "I thank the committee very much for their very nice selection of articles - JR." "Warmest thanks. Stra'ven can give every one the lead yet - BAF." "I must thank the committee for being so generous to the soldiers. The Stra'ven boys are keeping up the good name of Stra'ven here - WO." "I never appreciated anything like it before, as everything it contained is of the greatest use - JF." The following letter from Pte. James McKay dated 9th December is interesting: "I now take great pleasure in writing to thank the committee for parcel. It came just at a very useful time when we retired to a village for a rest which we were very much in need of. After being in the trenches for about three months, it is quite a change to get under a roof and have a good night's rest without any fears of shells bursting over your head as they are very unpleasant to listen to. I often wonder what the people at home would say if they saw us coming from the trenches needing a wash and a shave. There are some fine sights! One thing I must say is that is that the people here are very good. They allow us the use of their houses for cooking etc. As I sit and write, the old lady and gent are sitting at the fire talking together in their own language. It seems funny to hear them when you cannot understand . It is a great pity to see some of the towns that have been wrecked by the Germans. We came through one the other night that had been shelled shortly before then. It was burning away and nobody there to stop it. Another awful thing is to see all the poor people with their children fleeing from home terror stricken. The German's are an awful lot when they go into any places. What is of no use to them they destroy. Things seem to be very quiet for now. We have heard no guns going for a day or two unless they are performing for some new move or other. they have had some hard trials to break through our lines but all in vain. It is nearly always night work they go in for but no good as they see the bayonet they draw back again afraid for the steel of French's (Sir John French's) contemptible little army as they call it - JMcA."*

Issue Saturday, 26th December, 1914.

The Refugees:

Another burden - the Belgian Refugees, has been cast upon the shoulders of the British people by the war, and it must be said that they have accepted the charge nobly. Towns and cities, villages and country districts have taken in and cared for the poor Belgian refugees that have sought shelter among us. Thousands of poor people in many cases starving and friendless have rushed from the Germans to seek a home among us. The Refugee Committee has succoured and helped these poor people and done as much as it can to make things a little better for them. Besides the very poor, who in many cases were wealthy a few weeks ago, there are many who managed to bring a little money and these have settled among us waiting until it will be safe for them to return to their native land while their husbands and brothers are fighting. Among the strange sights to be seen in London are Belgian papers printed in Flemish and French and sold in the streets of London by refugee news girls.

Survey of 1914:

In these concluding days of the year, it is difficult to cast the eye backward to any other event than the World War which began in August of 1914. Yet the events of the seven opening months of the year judged on ordinary conditions were unusually important and interesting. After the outbreak of war, public interest concentrated on military and naval affairs and all events not directly in line with them were relegated to the background. Sport of all kinds is practically at a standstill, and Association Football, though still played by professional teams, holds a mere shadow of is former importance. Similarly music, the drama, everything which usually goes to make up the winter's indoor interest is practically non-existent. Britain is a nation of warring men and women, and anything not leading either directly to victory by land or sea or to the amelioration of preventing all hardship among those left behind is looked upon askance.

Hamilton Advertiser

Issue: Saturday, 16th January, 1915.

Shocking Accident:

On Thursday a boy named McLeavy residing in North Street fell down between the Crown Hall and the Gospel Hall and was impaled on a railing spike. The spike speared into his stomach seriously injuring him and his recovery is doubtful. It appears that there is a regular practice amongst youngsters of frequenting this place in the hope of picking up scraps of films discarded in the Picture House and this was the lad's intention. He was removed to the infirmary.

Issue: Saturday, 23rd January, 1915.

Clothing for Belgian Refugees - An appeal:

Another large party of Belgian Refugees arrived in Glasgow last week, and have now all been distributed throughout the various districts in Scotland. The providing of these people with clothes has been a very severe tax on the Glasgow store situated at 27 Cadogan Street. The articles left on hand are quite inadequate to meet the demand. In addition to providing for the new-comers the ladies in charge had that much of the clothing distributed in October and November is becoming worn out, and in many cases there is a demand to refit the people who have been in our midst for some time. The committee earnestly appeal for further contributions. The following articles are particularly required:- Costumes and waterproofs of large size, underclothing of all descriptions, night-dresses, handkerchiefs, and boots of large size for ladies; nightdresses for children, and boys' suits and complete suits for men, underwear of good quality, handkerchiefs and boots of large size. The boots required are nearly all exceptionally large, and the committee find that they seldom get sizes large enough to suit many of the men. Therefore, they would be pleased to receive money gifts to enable them to purchase where necessary. Friends will probably be aware that Glasgow is the distributing centre of the refugees for all Scotland, which means there is a constant heavy drain upon the Glasgow store.

Belgian Relief:

Attention is drawn to the notice in the advertising column calling a public meeting on Tuesday first of farmers and others to arrange for an auction of gifts of cattle, farming and dairy produce, and other articles, following the example of other districts. For instance, Cumnock in this way has raised over £700, Stranraer over £1000, and Castle Douglas over £2000. It is hoped that there will be a large turnout of the farmers and of the public generally, and that the response will be very liberal. It may be mentioned that a number of townspeople have been for some time maintaining five families of Belgian refugees numbering thirty people in furnished houses in Strathaven which have been been lent gratuitously. Not a great many people so far have contributed to this fund, but the committee, in addition to receiving donations of single payments, have been in receipt of a steady income from sums ranging of 1s to £1 per week, and also of several small weekly payments from factory workers, and their funds have also been supplemented by receipts from public entertainments. Many gifts of clothing have also been received, and four farmers have sent gifts of potatoes, while two farmers are making a weekly cash contribution. Three of the five Belgian families have two members working, and the other two have one member working. The committee have allowed those working to retain 25 per cent of their earnings, and the balance is being applied in reducing the cost of maintenance of the families. The committee are building up a substantial reserve fund, but, after April, they will require to pay rents for most of the furnished houses, and it is their intention, when the refugees depart, to give them a money payment to assist them in making a new start in life. Any surplus will be applied to relieving distress in Belgium. The Parish Church congregation have also just arranged to have a retiring collection each Sunday to raise funds for maintaining more refugees here or for sending assistance to Belgium direct. The local Refugee Committee have, in response to the appeal made at the public meeting held in Glasgow on Wednesday, informed the Glasgow Corporation that they are willing to provide accommodation and to maintain other two families. A great many well-to do people in Strathaven have, so far, taken little or no interest in the matter, and it is hope that they will embrace the opportunity which the proposed sale will afford them of contributing substantially like so many other people all over the world towards relieving the appalling distress of the Belgian people. Shopkeepers are specially invited to contribute gifts of goods. One well-known farmer has promised to give a pedigree bull stirk, and several other donations of farm stock and produce have already been promised.

Accident to a Boy:

We are pleased to report that the accident which happened to the lad McLeavy at the Picture House on Friday last has turned out less serious than was at first expected and that he is now going on very well.

Issue: Saturday, 13th February, 1915.

The Late Mr James Gebbie of Netherfield:

On Friday there passed away at Prince's Hotel, Bournemouth, one of Strathaven's best known men in the person of Mr. James Gebbie of Netherfield, Strathaven, the respected head of the well-known firm of Gebbie & Wilson, writers. Mr. Gebbie was a son of Mr. William Gebbie who was the first writer in Strathaven, and was born in 1834. He was educated at the legal profession at Glasgow University, and on the death of his father in 1865 he continued the extensive law business which had been carried on by his father since 1816. In 1898 he assumed as a partner Mr. John Wilson, writer, and thereafter carried on business under the firm name of Gebbie & Wilson until his retirement eighteen months ago. From an early period in his life he took a keen and active interest in all matters appertaining to the welfare of his native town, and served with distinction on the old Parochial Board, retaining his connection with the change to Parish Council, when he became the first chairman of the latter body. He also had a long connection with the Heritors' Committee, and for many years has been chairman. A number of years' service were also give on the School Board. Mr. Gebbie's abilities as a lawyer were well known and he had many honours conferred upon him, the principal of which were the appointment of Clerk of the Peace for the Middle Ward of Lanarkshire and Dean of Faculty for Lanarkshire. For the last twenty years Mr. Gebbie's activities have been somewhat limited owing to the delicate state of his health, and latterly he has been compelled to winter in more southern latitudes. His interest in Strathaven, however, has never lessened and on all occasions of public effort his sympathy and practical help has always been forthcoming. Mr. Gebbie's family consisted of three sons and one daughter, and it was our painful duty some weeks ago to record the fact that one of his sons was killed in action in France. Mrs Gebbie pre-deceased her husband some two years ago, thus the surviving members of the family are two sons and a daughter, for whom in this time of bereavement much sympathy is felt. The funeral took place on Wednesday from the East United Free Church, in the hall of which the body lay overnight. The funeral service was taken part in by Rev. A.W. Donaldson, B.A., John Muirhead, B.D., and Matthew Urie Baird and the Dead March in Saul was played as the coffin was taken out. The coffin was an oak one, and was covered with wreaths sent by friends in the district and including a floral tribute of sympathy from Lord and Lady Newlands. To the tolling of the bell, the cortege made its way to the graveyard, here the last rites were performed by Rev. Robert Paterson, M.A., Glassford.

Issue: Saturday, 20th February, 1915

War Relief Funds:

The Farmers of the district are to be congratulated on the splendid generosity which has marked the appeal made to them for free gifts on behalf of the War Relief Funds. Not only have they given freely themselves but they have canvassed their friends to good advantage with the result that there is a catalogue of over sixteen pages being a list of cattle, sheep, pigs, poultry, dairy produce, farm implements, cheese, butter, eggs etc offered for sale. The livestock will be sold at the Strathaven Auction Market in the morning and the goods which appeal to the housewife will be sold in the Public Hall in the afternoon at two. We presume that many housewives will take the opportunity of doing their shopping for goods of undoubted quality and attend for this weekend at the Public Hall where they will be certain to get the same time to help a good cause. A certain amount of mystery surrounds the announcement that the 'Kaiser' is to be sold at the mart in the morning. All that is wanted now is buyers, and we hope that they will be forthcoming in good numbers at both sales.

Issue: Saturday, 27th February, 1915.

The War Plough:

Rev. James Ferguson's Thoughtful

Address

The annual weekly intercessory meeting of the Hamilton Churches was held jointly with the monthly meeting of the Laymen's Missionary Movement on Wednesday evening in the Baptist Church. Mr John Ballantyne presided over a goodly turnout representative of the different congregations in the town, and on the platform with him were the Revs. James Ferguson, Crieff (formerly of Hamilton), J. McGibbon, T. M. B Paterson, J. McCallum Robertson, C. Inglis Wardrop, J. A. Lees, J. Murphy, and J. Bell Johnston. The opening proceedings were taken part in by the Revs. J. Mc. C. Robertson and J. McGibbon, and Messrs W. J. Whiting and R. Gibson.

The speaker for the evening was the Rev. James Ferguson, whose subject was, "The Plough of War in the Field of the World." If they were to go into the country, he said, they would find men and horses busy in the fields, and they might even think that, by the overturning of the grass with the clovers and daisies, the beauty of nature was being destroyed. It was when they thought of the rich crop that their hearts went out in hope for the plentiful harvest. Was not, he asked, war like a great plough tearing up the soil of modern life in Europe and further field? The plough of war had torn up their lea-land, and was driving the iron right into the meadow land of their pleasure- loving life. Under their long material prosperity they were settling down to think that the one thing desirable was to lie on a back of peaceful wealth and listen to the larks, or mayhap make daisy chains or chase the butterflies. All that had been rudely shaken by the war. They were breaking through the surface of their life, and the war had turned up the rich red soil underneath.

The truth had been driven into their minds that there were things more essential than commercial success, social distinction, and personal ease. They were forced to a consideration of the deeper facts of life and death. To man, preoccupied with material things, there had come an upheaval, in which the spiritual factors of life had been brought to light. This change, he went on to say, was reflected in the leading journals of the daily press, where of a morning, instead of the usual editorials, they found sermons on such texts as *"Right is Might." "What shall it profit a man to gain the whole world and lose his own soul?" "Righteousness alone exalted a Nation,"* etc., Their ideas of civilisation had also been changed, and they had been forced to think of what lay below the surface. It had been driven home that, if civilisation and education, outward equipment of life, the discipline of the intellect even, had not the renewing spirit of Christ in it, then it was only a sweeping and garnishing of the life. The ultimate question of all culture and civilisation was what spirit possessed it. The type of civilisation which they as Christians must look for was that which was mystically set forth in the Christian Apocalypse under the figure of a New Jerusalem wherein there entered nothing that defiled or worked abomination or market a lie. On the question of peace, also, their hopes had been radically turned over. With all their talk and aspirations, all their sanguine expectations that a day of universal peace would come, they had no guarantee of peace except as the nations of the world were exercised by a high sense of honour and the recognition of the rights of people, great and small. It was only when the life of man was inspired by Jesus Christ that international peace was guaranteed. The moral sense of the world had been stirred in this crisis as they never remembered seeing it stirred before, and in this connection the speaker referred his audience to the articles that were appearing the leading journals all over the world. But upheaval, he went on to say in conclusion, was not in itself a blessing. Man ploughed not merely to cut up the sweet earth, but to prepare it for the sewer. In these days of war the rich land had been turned up, and if they could see any evidence, under the providence of God, of its being turned to good account, let them give thanks. By this upheaval the fruits of life would be richer and the harvest more abundant. But it lay with Christian men all over thru world to seize the opportunity, if they desired to reap the fruits that had been thrown into the earth prepared to receive it. The Chairman, in name of all present, conveyed to Mr Ferguson their hearty thanks for his thoughtful and inspirational address.

Issue Saturday, 6th March, 1915.

Advertisement:

Men Wanted - Recruits are Urgently Required for the 8th Battalion Highland Light Infantry

Foreign Service Enlist now at Headquarters, Hope Street, Lanark.

Patriotic Pageant: "The Allies"

A patriotic pageant under the above title was produced by the sisters of our soldiers and Boy Scouts in the Public Hall, on Thursday evening. Mr. James Cameron, C.C., presided, and the hall was quite filled. The opening tableau was Britannia, who called upon the Home Countries, to which England, Scotland, Ireland and Wales responded. Each country was represented by a young lady in national costume accompanied by a Boy Scout. Interesting poetic references to the past history of the countries were recited by the boys, followed by the singing of National Anthems or airs by the ladies. At the close of the scene, a hymn, "Lord while for all mankind we pray," was sung by the entire company, followed by a tableau "The Home Counties." Scene II. opened with "Belgium Prostrate," a striking group with two Belgian soldiers in the forefront and a woman in the costume and attitude of despair in the background. Appropriate reference was made, after which the curtain dropped to rise again on the animated scene of "Belgian Resurgens" - a group of Belgian refugees in the national dress, who sang the National Anthem, "La Brabanconne." European Allies and Japan were next called in, the representatives singing the National Anthems. This scene closed with a hymn for the Allies. Scene III. opened with the singing of "Ye Mariners of England." Britannia then calling upon the colonies. Immediately followed a pathetic tableau - a local soldier who has lost a leg being seen lying wounded on the battlefield with an angel standing guard over him. The chant of the Boy Scouts and a recitation "The appeal of the Sisters of our Soldiers" comprised the fine scene. Space forbids a more detailed description, but in generalising we may say that the production was masterly and the groupings and tableaux beyond all praise. Too high a compliment cannot be paid to the gifted authoress, Mrs. Dey. M.A., Rankin Manse, for the really class poetry contained in the passages recited by the boys, and the ideas so splendidly carried out in the groupings and tableaux; whilst to one and all of the numerous performers we heartily say "well done." Miss Helen F. Shearer, who acted as accompanist, had a lot of work to get through and she did her part well, the accompaniments being sympathetic and well timed. It was suggested at the close that the piece might be re-produced in the neighbouring towns, and should this be given effect to we have no hesitation in recommending it as an entertainment which is well worthy of being attended. The object of the production was to raise money for the local relief funds.

Issue: Saturday, 13th March, 1915.

Local Belgian Refugee Committee:

This committee, in view of the allocation of £100 to its funds by the committee in connection with the Farmers Free Gift Sale have intimated to the Glasgow Corporation that they are willing to take other twelve refugees in addition to the thirty-four who are presently being maintained here. The committee are meantime endeavouring to secure furnished houses to accommodate these additional refugees, and also a family of above who are presently here and whose house will not be available after next month. They would also like to procure farm work for two male refugees presently here and for any others who may come and are fitted for such work.

Avendale Free Gift Sale:

At a largely attended meeting of committee on Tuesday it was reported that the net proceeds of the sale were fully £830, and after consideration the amount was allocated as follows: Distress in Belgium, £200; Local Belgian Refugees' Fund, £100; British Farmers' Red Cross Association, £50; Hillpark Home, Bothwell, £50; Local Red Cross Society, £50; Boy Scouts, £10; and the balance, £370, to the Avondale War Relief Fund to be dealt with as might be found desirable. Mr. Cameron, C.C., congratulated the committee on the wonderfully successful effort they had made and moved a vote of thanks to the Chairman, Mr. David Jack, Dykehead. The following gentlemen were nominated to the Avondale General Committee: Committee - Messrs David Jack, Dykehead; Alex Watt. Hillhead; P. McFarlane, Rigghead, Thomas Findlay, Floors; and James Young, Greenfield.

Strathaven Mutual Improvement Association:

The annual general meeting of the members of this association was held on the evening of Monday last in the Lesser Public Hall. The president, Mr J. McFarlane Paterson, occupied the chair. A financial statement was submitted by the treasurer which showed that the sum of £15.10s.6d had been handed over to Avondale War Relief Fund. The statement showed a loss of £5.11s.8d on the working for the year; while the balance at the credit of the association is now £10.5s.7d The statement was unanimously adopted. The following were elected to the Board of Management:- President, Mr Wm. Watt, jeweller; vice-president, Mr James Lothian, secretary, Mr Wm. Renfrew; treasurer, Mr Wm. Riddell; committee, Misses Dougan, J. Shearer and Wilson. Messrs Thomas Hamilton, J. McFarlane, Paterson, Matthew, Semple, and Miss Smith.

Issue: Saturday, 20th March, 1915.

Dancing:

Miss Muir's classes reopen on Tuesday first in Public Hall.

A Fatal Fall:

Mr. Alexander Shearer, boot and shoemaker, Waterside Street was accidentally killed by falling down the stairs at his own house on Wednesday evening. He had been on a visit to some friends in Larkhall and returned by the 9.30 train. He appeared to be all right till he reached home and there as stated he fell on the stairs and when picked up was found to be dead. For some considerable time Mr. Shearer had been in poor health and was subject to heart turns. He leaves a widow and a daughter.

Belgian Refugees:

The committee invites offers of furnished houses for the accommodation of refugees during the summer - reply stating particulars and rents. J. Torrance, Secretary.

Issue: Saturday, 27th March, 1915.

Proceeds of Pageant:

From the patriotic pageant "The Allies" which was produced at Strathaven on March 4th, Mrs. Dey has been able to hand over a sum of £13.10s to the Treasurer of the War Relief Fund. The pageant will be repeated in Stonehouse on Friday, 2nd April.

St. Patrick's Congregational Gathering:

A social in honour of St.Patrick was held in the hall of St. Patrick's Chapel on the evening of Friday last. Rev. Father O'Leary presided, supported by Messrs. Mulligan and McLeavy. After an enjoyable tea purveyed by Mr Taylor, a grand programme was sustained by the more musically inclined of the congregation. The entertainment itself was quite a "surprise packet" the manner in which the various artistes comported themselves being almost equal to that of professionals. The audience was the largest for quite a long time, owing among other things, to the presence of several Belgian refugees who were the guests of the evening. The following ladies and gentlemen contributed to the harmony of the evening:- Messrs. Dempsey, Horan, Cytha, Casey and Mademoiselles Rothern, and Vanderheyden. Messrs. McLeavy, Mulligan, Cassidy, Campbell, Dempsey and the harmony of the gathering - the evening concluded with votes of thanks and the singing of "God Save Ireland."

Comforts for Belgians:

It will be recollected that a Working Party organised by Mrs. Watt. Greenside, sent a consignment of comforts for destitute Belgians in the month of September last. These have been acknowledged this week in the following terms "Belgian Relief Fund" Millen House, 8/9 Chiswell Street, London, E.C. - *"19th March, 1915.Dear Madam, referring to the generous gift of socks which you so kindly sent several months ago for the benefit of the Belgian refugees, I am sure you will like to hear how much they have been appreciated. The box was sent to Belgium where so many thousands of my poor countrymen are still in need of every necessity of life including clothing. The gifts were distributed where distress was greatest and were received with the greatest gratitude. Will you kindly convey my heartfelt thanks to all the kind friends in your town who have so generously contributed to the gift. The socks proved most acceptable. I am still forwarding consignments of clothing every week for distribution both in Holland and in Belgium where the distress is, unfortunately, still very acute. Again thank you for your kindness. Yours very faithfully, J. Navaue. P.S. The milk jug covers proved most useful."*

Issue: Saturday, 17th April, 1915.

Scottish Patriots Concert:

We are pleased to notice from advertisement that the clever Scottish composer Mr. Robert Machardy is to give a concert in the Public Hall on Monday evening. On former occasions we have endeavoured to draw attention to the claims of this native musical genius, but fear that he has to a great extent experienced the truth of the scriptures in that "a prophet hath not honour in his own land". Recent events, however, seem to have put a different complexion on many things, and it is to be hoped that this extends to things musical and that the easy-going British public is now to make amends for its worshipping at the shrine of the foreign musicians by paying a little more attention to native talent. Dr. Machardy has collected a galaxy of talent for Monday evening's concert and we feel sure that those who attend are in for a treat. In honour of our brave sons who have gone to the front at this time, Dr. Machardy has composed a military march "Heroes of Avondale" and with the assistance of an orchestra this piece will be given at concert.

Issue: Saturday, 22nd May, 1915.

Prisoner of War:

Mrs Coats, Crosshill Farm, has received a postcard from her son Private Robert Coats, 48th Highlanders of Canada, in which he states that he is wounded and a prisoner of war. The post-card is marked Kniegdaz, but it is not known whether he is imprisoned there or posted the card as he passed through. The nature of the wound is not stated but he mentions that he is "getting on all right."

Issue: Saturday, 29th May, 1915.

Help Gallant Little Serbia:

Today, in common with most places in the district, Strathaven is having a Flag Day on behalf of Serbia. We commend the effort to the sympathetic support of the public. The part that Serbia has played in the present great crisis has to a considerable extent been overshadowed by the records of the deeds of and suffering of nations nearer home, but it is nevertheless quite as valuable. Chosen by Austria-Hungary as the object of her wrath over the murder of the Prince Francis Ferdinand, the invasion of Serbia became the "casus belle" of the European conflict and the peculiar turn of events and combination of opposing forces worked out in such a manner that this country was probably saved from a future war of single combat with Germany - a contingent she would probably have been unable to face. A result of the war has been the wholesale spread of disease in Serbia, the ravishes of which, owing to lack of hospital accommodation etc., are inestimable and the proceeds of today's Flag Day will be used to relieve this distress. It will be remembered that a former Strathaven District Nurse - Nurse Jordan - has already laid down her life in Serbia in helping to fight the fell diseases which have arisen. Another member of the brave band of nurses writes *"she was passionately devoted to her work and was loved very dearly by all those in our party."* It is hoped that the Strathaven Flag Day will be a worthy tribute to her memory.

Obituary:

The public who do business at the Post Office will mourn with regret the death of Miss May Morton which took place in Glasgow on Tuesday. Miss Morton had gone to the city to undergo an operation but it was unsuccessful. A woman of cheery nature and even temperament, Miss Morton was greatly liked by the business public and will be much missed. She was a member of the Rankin United Free Church and a willing worker in the various activities of this Church.

Issue: Saturday, 12th June, 1915.

Serbian Flag Day:

Grateful acknowledgement has been received for the handsome sum of £41.15.3d collected in Strathaven and Avondale for Serbia & The Scottish Women's Hospitals on 29th May. Special thanks are due the Lady Collectors assisted by the Boy Scouts for their enthusiastic and successful work despite the unfortunate weather.

Issue: Saturday, 19th June, 1915.

Presentation:

On Tuesday evening employees of Messrs. Elder & Watson, Dunlop Street, Hosiery Factory met honour to Mr. James Glass on the occasion of his marriage and presented him with a handsome barometer. Mr. Tobert J. Elder made the presentation, and in a few words conveyed the good wishes of the employees. Mr. Glass suitably replied and expressed his appreciation of the gift.

Accident:

On Thursday evening a young Belgian woman named Sidomie Vanderheyden was cycling along Green Street when near Walker's Bridge she knocked down and ran over a lad of about eight years of age named Scobbie the son of visitors residing in Green Street. The little chap appeared to be pretty badly hurt about the face. He was carried to Greenside Dispensary where he was attended to by Dr. Alan Watt and afterwards carried home. Practically at the same time a boy named William Craig coming off Lethame Road on a bicycle rode into Mr. David Cassels, blacksmith, who was proceeding towards Green Street from Townhead Street on his bicycle, three cyclists were thrown off their machines but fortunately neither suffered injury. The bicycles were damaged.

A Brave Cameron:

Information has reached Mrs. Hendry, 39 Bellfield Street, Dennistoun, that her son, Pte. Alexander Hendry of the 2nd Cameron Highlanders, has died from wounds. Lieut. B.D. Wylie commanding D Company, wrote to Mrs. Hendry, in a sympathetic letter, that her son was shot about the legs very badly by shrapnel and died of his wounds. Sergt. Major McCallum, of 'B' Company in which Pte. Hendry served, wrote *"The cheery nature of your son made him always a welcome companion with the other men, and I assure you they will miss him very much. When he started to do duty in the trenches he was soon recognised by his officers, commissioned and non-commissioned as being always keen to undertake any duty, however dangerous or difficult, and was consistently often entrusted with such duties as . . . and the carrying of messages to and from the firing line, his hardihood and nerve carrying him through when other men gave up. He had been offered stripes several times but preferred to remain a private in the ranks."* Pte Hendry, who accompanied his regiment to France in December, had been in the trenches since the beginning of January. His brother, William, is a trooper in the Queen's Own Glasgow Yeomanry. Pte. Hendry is a grandson of Mr and Mrs. Reid, Barn Street, Strathaven.

Issue: Saturday, 26th June, 1915.

Promotion:

Congratulations to our townsman, Mr David McKay, on his promotion to Sergeant Major of 3/6th Scottish Rifles. He was on duty with the recruiting party in the G.A.P.P. on Saturday.

British Women's Temperance Association:

At the Cattle Show on June 9th, the members of the British Women's Temperance Association ran a most successful tea tent. During the whole of the day, the tent with its flags and motto, its flowers, its beautifully set tables, and excellent service was a centre of attraction for visitors who several times tested its capacity to overflowing. After paying all accounts the ladies have had the pleasure of handing a donation of £2 to the secretary of the local Belgian Relief Fund.

Heritors of Avondale:

A general meeting was held in the Parish Church, Strathaven - Mr John S. Napier, J.P., in the chair. Mr Napier made reference to the loss sustained by the heritors on the death of Mr James Gebbie who for about 30 years had been their convener and whose services were so much appreciated.

Strathaven and the War:

Pte. William Howat, 2nd Seaforth Highlanders, was killed in the trenches in France, and the manner in which he met his death is told in the appended letter from a chum to Mrs Alexander Watson, with whom he lodged prior to his enlistment. Pte. Howat was a son of the late Mr Gavin Howat, postman, and served his time in the tailoring trade in the Co-operative Society's tailoring department. He was a quiet, smart lad, and much thought of by those who knew him:- "*It is with deepest regret that I inform you of Willie Howat's death. He and about eight of his comrades were killed by the one shell while in the trenches. Willie was a good pal to me, and I miss him as you and his relations will. He was the last of my four chums. I am the only one left out of five, and my turn may come any moment, but I pray to God that I may be spared to come back alive. If you have one of Willie's photos, I would be very glad to have it in remembrance of an old comrade.*" - We regret also to learn of the death of Pte. Peter Saunders, Scots Guards, who, before the outbreak of war, was employed with Mr James P. Morrison, ironmonger, Commongreen. Saunders was not a local lad, but during his stay here made many friends, and was engaged to a local girl. He was a fine big robust fellow, and looked the typical guardsman.

Lance-Corporal Joseph Brownlie of "D" Coy., 6TH Battalion Scottish Rifles, was wounded in the recent engagement in France and is in hospital.

The Late Lieutenant Wilson:

We regret to report the death of Second-Lieutenant John B. Wilson, 6th Battalion the Cameronians (Scottish Rifles), in an attack on the German trenches in France. He was the only son of Mr John Wilson, writer, and was 21 years of age. Lieutenant Wilson was well-known in the community, having been educated at Crosshill School and Hamilton Academy, and was held in the highest esteem by all who knew him. He was studying law at Glasgow University and was in the office of Messrs Maclay, Murray & Spens, writers, Glasgow. He had served two years in the University Training Corps, and on the outbreak of war he accepted a commission in the 6th Scottish Rifles, and has been with the battalion since August last, being attached to 'D' Company. Particulars of his death are given in the following letter from his senior officer, Major W. S. McKenzie, to his father:- *"The report of Jack's death came to me as a terrible shock, in spite of the fact that any one who came out alive from that zone of shell fire and bullets would perform a miracle. The last time I saw him he was in his place leading on his men, and he beamed on me as I passed in his natural cheerful manner. We made an attack on the German lines and our battalion was chosen for the assault. For some time beforehand our artillery severely bombarded the position. We were the third Company to advance, and we got over the parapet and commenced our part of the target. The space between our parapet and that of the Germans' was by this time a perfectly shower-splattered plain of shrapnel and bullets. Yet the advance never hesitated. Our particular objective was some fortified houses on the other side of the German lines. Jack's was the second platoon of my Company, and as I was rushing on to the front platoon I passed Jack on the way, and it was then I last saw him, behaving like a veteran and a hero, and perfectly cool. He smiled a friendly recognition as I passed, and shortly thereafter I was hit with shrapnel on the head. For a time I was knocked out being rendered insensible. The report as to the behaviour of Jack and what was left of his platoon came to me afterwards, and what consolation there is to you may be got from the undernoted fact that he did all that was expected of him. He and a few men actually reached the objective - those houses. If I could describe to you what that meant, with guns bursting at ten yards interval, and in different places each time, literally covering the field with shrapnel, having not a foot that was not affected, and added to this the scream of rifle bullets as they spat into us in thousands, I could give you some idea of the bravery, the determination, that sense of duty and patriotism which enabled him and his men to reach those houses. When he got there he was shot by a rifle bullet. He was killed instantaneously, and would suffer no pain. Although we captured the German position we could not hold it. A retiral was therefore made to our own lines again. We will all miss Jack. I especially. He was such a favourite. Always in good humour, ready for action at all times, at all hours, and as our Adjutant once remarked to me, a good officer. I cannot yet realise he is gone. I wish I could say or do something to alleviate your loss. I cannot except that I might say you are not to forget that he died doing his duty, his "bit for home and fatherland. Yours in the sacrifice: his the gain.* Private A. McCallum of Strathaven, who was with Lieutenant Wilson, reports that he was killed on spot just as he was giving an order to an N.C.O. in his platoon. He adds, *"In him we have lost a good fellow and one who was respected and liked by the men under his charge."*

An Appreciation

"To his relative and friends Lieutenant Wilson's passing away means the blighting of many hopes, and the loss of a personality that was ever brave, winsome, genial, and chivalrous. In his various classes at school and the University he showed himself a thorough painstaking student, winning many prizes, and above all and beyond all the affection and esteem of his fellow students. A useful prosperous career was opening out before him when the call came to serve king and country in the greatest war of the centuries. He at once obeyed. On the evening of the fatal day he was leading his men - who loved him dearly and would have followed him anywhere upon the German trenches when he fell mortally wounded. And lo! In a moment "he was not for God took him." He was indeed "a very perfect, gentle knight," a Sir Galahad among young men.

Issue: Saturday, 3rd July, 1915.

Strathaven Scholars at Hamilton Academy:

We are pleased to learn of the success of local scholars as under:- Dux Medal for girls, and medal for Scottish History, Jean Riddell, Kirk Street; Burns' Medal - Catherine Hamilton, Melbourne Cottage, Ballgreen; class prize, John Stirling, Hamilton Road; Gymnastics Medal - George Allan, Overton Road.

Strathaven and the War:

Stravonians will learn with pride that the Distinguished Conduct Medal has been conferred on Company Sergeant-Major George Young, Queen's Own Cameron Highlanders. The Sergeant-Major is a son of the late tenant of Newton Farm. As a lad he was apprenticed to the drapery trade with Mr James Allan (now William Tennent), Commongreen, and afterwards was in business for himself. Later he exchanged the yard stick for the rifle, and in the Cameron Highlanders has proved himself to be a splendid soldier. He has been with his regiment in India, and about a year ago was home for a time on furlough. His future career will be watched with increased interest.

Sergeant James Anderson, No. 1 Coy., 13th Battalion, 3rd Brigade Canadian Contingent, Royal Highlanders of Canada, a son of the late Mr James Anderson, slater and plasterer, Todshill, favours us with the appended letter:- *Dear Friend, - I write you seeing you are one of the old Scottish Rifles men to let you know I am in the pink of condition and still going strong. I may say that my training in the Ranks has stood me in good shape since our battle at Ypres. I have come through it all and have seen a bit of life. Our second battle was at Festubert where we had to go through hell. That is what I call it. To support an attack with comrades falling right and left was awful, but still we went on under heavy shell fire. We gained our point and held our trench for three days, when we were released by another battalion. Coming out of that trench a considerable thunderstorm came on, and the enemies started to fly. Such a night! I will never forget it as long as I live. We got back half strength. We lost our officers, and I, being the only sergeant in the platoon, had to handle the men just the same. That is where my past training came in. I hear some Strathaven boys have got knocked over. Old Strathaven has done her bit for the country. Good luck to the old home town. I suppose there will be very few of the old boys to be seen in the town. A quiet life for me after . . "*

Issue: Saturday, 10th July, 1915.

Gifts for Soldiers:

The employees of Messrs Elder & Watson, Dunlop Street, have despatched their second consignment of "packed" socks, and Major Dykes acknowledges same and undertakes to forward them to the men of the 6th Scottish Rifles in active service. "Packed" it might be explained is that each girl takes home a pair of socks and puts inside them such gifts as cigarettes, tobacco, sweetmeats etc., and encloses her name and address. Many interesting communications have been received from soldiers of the previous consignment.

Issue: Saturday, 17th July, 1915.

Strathaven Soldier in German West Africa:

The following letter is from Trooper James M. Summers, 4th S.A. Mounted Rifles, a son of Mr Wm. Summers, Newton Road. The titanic struggle in Europe is to a great extent overshadowing the operations elsewhere, and the news from other parts is meagre. The letter of Trooper Summers will, therefore, be read with all the more interest:- *"We had a safe passage up to G.S.W., and gave our horses a rest for about two weeks. Then we started, and I can tell you we have done some tramping, We had a fight at a place called Bethsheba and beat them back and took the town. I must say we were very lucky, only losing a few men. Then we chased them on to a place called Gibaon where there is a German artillery barracks, and they were reinforced. We had a hot time of it for a bit. We practically rode into a trap, and they opened fire on us with their big guns, pom poms and maxims about 2.30 in the morning, but we got out of it, only we lost 30 men and 65 wounded. Well, we rode off for a little distance, and waited until daylight, then we attacked them and beat them, chasing them 30 miles, and would have captured the lot, only our horses were dead beat and they had fresh horses, so we had to let them go. Anyhow we took over 300 prisoners and captured 3 of their big* *guns, one pom pom, and 7 maxims, so we did not do so bad. It's the biggest scrap there has been up here so far. I was lucky enough to get through without a scratch, only I was pretty well knocked-up, as we were in the saddle for 18 hours out of the 24 for over two weeks. I am with the 4th Mounted Rifles, and we are with the central forces under Sir Duncan Mackenzie. We are the flying column, and you have got to go when you are with him. He is a proper mad Scotchman, but he is a good man . Well, General Botha has taken Winakook, and the Germans have retired leaving all their women and children, and have gone to the Waterberg Mountains about 400 miles further north. We are at present about 120 miles from Winakook, and are taking it in easy stages as we are all in rags now and waiting to be rigged out again. This country is no good for anything, only diamonds. We came over 300 miles with only one water bottle full of water allowed to us a day. In fact, I was more sorry for the poor horses than ourselves. Nothing but sand and desert till we got up to about Bethany, then it got a bit better. Now we are riding along the Fish River, and we get plenty of water and wood, but our transport is rotten. We were living on nothing but mutton and water for a month, and a lot of chaps got laid up with dysentery. I had a slight touch, but nothing serious. Well, mother, it is very kind of them at home to send me out a parcel, but I have not received it yet. In fact, I have had them sent from Natal and never received them, but that is a common complaint here. The transport department is rotten. We have not had a full week's rations issued out to us since we left the base about two months ago."*

Issue: Saturday, 24th July, 1915.

"The Kaiser":

That well known donkey, "The Kaiser" which, at the free gift sale held on February last realised the handsome sum of £50, was exposed for sale at Strathaven Auction Market on Tuesday last. There was a large attendance in the Sale Ring on Tuesday, and after being sold upwards of 50 times, the total realised was £18. This sum given to the Red Cross Society.

Issue: Saturday, 31st July, 1915.

Anniversary of Declaration of War:

Attention is called to the intercessory service to be held in the East Church on Wednesday evening first. Services such as these will be held in all the Allied countries, and it is hoped that there will be a large gathering at the service to be held in Strathaven. The local minister will lead the service.

East Church Jubilees:

The "Record of the United Free Church" for August has inserted a notice of the jubilee of Mr James Martin and Mr William Findlay as elders in the East United Free Church. Excellent photographs of the two aged elders, and of the Rev. Mr Donaldson are reproduced , and the magazine will form an interesting souvenir of the unique occasion.

Cycling Accident:

At the New Cross on Saturday evening Miss Bryson was run down by a man who came down Townhead Street at a terrific rate. He had apparently lost control, as he ran down the other cyclist practically on the pavement on his right. Miss Bryson's bicycle was badly smashed, but she herself escaped with some minor cuts on the arms. The male cyclist made off without giving an account of himself.

Cycling Accident:

At the New Cross on Thursday evening, Mrs Waddell was run down by a postman who came down Townhead Street. Mrs Waddell's bicycle was badly smashed, but she herself escaped serious injury.

Issue: Saturday, 14th August, 1915.

Station Burglary:

William Anderson, designed as a cattle drover of no fixed abode, was convicted at Hamilton on Thursday of having broken into the booking office at the Central Station, Strathaven, on 20th or 21st July, and stolen a silver albert, a metal badge, a hair comb, 2 pairs of window curtains, a screw driver, and a collection box containing 1/-. Accused admitted several previous convictions and was sentenced to six months imprisonment with hard labour. Hon. Sheriff Stodart occupied the Bench.

Local Soldiers:

Since writing last we have had the pleasure of travelling with Lieut. James Giffen, 2nd Battalion Cameron Highlanders who is presently superintending the training of machine gun teams at Invergordon. Of himself he has little to say, but of his fellow townsman, company Sergeant-Major George Young, he is full of praise. On the occasion when the Sergeant-Major won his D.C.M. Lieut. Giffen affirms that he saved the Division which was attacking. It happened thus:- Sergeant-Major Young was with the supports and had charge of a hut containing the supply of ammunition for the Division. One of his men accidentally upset a large tin pf petrol in the hut, and another who had been outside strolling in lighting a cigarette carelessly threw the match into the petrol. Flames burst up instantly. Sergeant-Major Young saw only one chance of saving the hut and its precious contents. He threw himself bodily on the flames and rolled over them till they were subdued. Surely no D.C.M. has been more worthily won! Quite a number of our younger soldiers who have joined since the outbreak of war have been home on leave during the past fortnight. In every case they are immensely improved with their training.

Issue: Saturday 21st August, 1915.

Midnight Marauders:

At the J.P. Court, Hamilton, on Monday, Mary Cameron or Welsh (66), vagrant, was fined 7s.6d, with the option of five days' imprisonment for creating a breach of the peace in Kirk Street at midnight on Saturday evening. An hour later Joseph McQueen, (59), labourer, was found in the same street hopelessly drunk. Queen was fined 10s, with the option of seven days' in prison.

Recruiting Meeting:

An open air recruiting meeting was held in the Commongreen on Friday evening last. County Councillor Cameron presided. There was a large gathering which listened to the addresses of Mr McEwan, Sheriff Campbell of Argyllshire and Major Wishart, officer in charge of the Hamilton recruiting area. The purpose of the gathering was not so much to get men on the spot as to tell them where and how to enlist. Votes of thanks were accorded on the call of the Rev. John Muirhead, B.D.

Obituary:

We regret to note the death of Mr William Findlay, Westfield Cottage which took place on Tuesday at the advanced age of 90. Mr Findlay was a weaver to trade, but also ran a successful grocery business in Barn Street for a number of years. In ordinary public matters he took little part, but in church affairs he was ever deeply interested. As a worker among the young he gave invaluable services to the East United Free Church, while in that congregation he was an elder for the long period of fully 50 years. Of a quiet nature, and gentle to a degree, Mr Findlay was beloved by all who knew him, and will be much missed.

Presentation:

The Corney Close Companions met in a social capacity in Taylor's Temperance Restaurant on Monday to honour Mr Andrew Brownlie, one of their number on the occasion of his marriage.

Mr James Brown occupied the chair and was supported on his right by Mr Brownlie, and on his left by Lieut. Shearer, 6th S.R. After a sumptuous repast, the Chairman, in his remarks, which were rich in humour, touched on their comrade's success since entering into partnership in the fleshing business, and was of opinion he would be quite a successful partner in the matrimonial profession. At an interval in the long musical programme which followed, the chairman called upon Mr Thomas Young to present Mr Brownlie with a very handsome kitchen clock of a plain but pretty design. Mr Young, in a few well-chosen words performed the presentation ceremony., and said he expressed the sentiments of the companions in wishing their chum and his good lady a long and prosperous married life.

Death of an Old Strathaven Lad on the Field of Honour:

Information has been received that John Richmond was killed in France by the bursting of a shell on the 6th August. Richmond learned the mason trade with the late Mr Allan senior, of the town, and 25 years ago he enlisted in the Argyll and Sutherland Highlanders, and gradually rose to the rank of sergeant. He saw service in India, being awarded the Indian Medal in 1895, also, the Punjab clasp, 1897-98, doing almost 13 years service with the colours, and four years in the Reserves. Immediately after the outbreak of war Sergeant Richmond re-joined the Army, and was appointed drill-instructor to Lochiel's Cameron's at Inverness, moving with the battalion first to Rushmoor Camp, then to Bramshot, and finally to Bristol, where they were stationed before crossing to France at the beginning of July. For the four years previous to his re-joining the army Sergeant Richmond was engaged as janitor at the Royal Technical College, Glasgow, where his obliging and tactful manner won the esteem of those with whom he came in contact. His Captain, in sending the information of his death, stated that he was second senior sergeant, and expressed his sympathies at the loss of a soldier with such a long and varied experience, which had been of great benefit to his company.

Sergeant William Hamilton Missing:

Information has been received that Sergeant William Hamilton, 4th Battalion Royal Fusiliers, was wounded on 16th June, and has been missing since that date. Sergeant Hamilton, who is a son of the late William Hamilton, formerly of Netherfield Farm, and grandson of the late Gavin Wear, Commercial Mills, Strathaven, enlisted in October last, and was sent to France in February, being at Ypres from then till 15th June. He was promoted sergeant and recommended for the D.C.M. for special services. In a letter received from one of his comrades, those services are described as follows:- *"One day, in the front line of trenches, the German artillery was shelling us heartily whilst our own was not replying. An officer tried to phone to our artillery, but the wires had been cut. Willie volunteered to carry a message back to our Battalion Headquarters, who would telephone the artillery. This meant a journey of two or three miles in broad daylight. He had to go across country, some hundreds of yards of which was bullet swept. At times he had to crawl along in the mud, but otherwise he was nearly up to the neck in mud and water, added to this he was sniped at from some distance. But he got there, and our artillery soon announced his arrival. He came back to the trench when darkness had fallen, having more than earned his presentation.*

Issue: Saturday, 28th August, 1915.

Home from the Front:

Nurse Harriet Thomson, Viewpark, who has been actively engaged in nursing work with the British army in France for a year, has been ordered home for a visit, and arrived last week. The twelve months have been a time of strenuous work, at many times under very unfavourable conditions, and we understand that Nurse Thomson is suffering from rheumatism as the result of exposure and dampness. Otherwise she is looking as bright and charming as ever.

Issue: Saturday, 4th September, 1915.

Belgian Refugees:

The local committee brought fourteen additional refugees to the district yesterday. Eight of those have been accommodated at Drumclog in a house kindly lent by Mr Daniel Smith, contractor, The family who formerly occupied Mr Smith's house left a short time ago to take up a small poultry farm in the United States. The local committee gave them a grant of £12. The Glasgow Corporation are urging the committee to find accommodation for more refugees, and the committee will be pleased to have offers of house accommodation. As will be seen from our advertising column, the committee are also appealing for donations of money and clothing The committee are about to publish a balance sheet to date.

Shooting Match:

On Saturday afternoon a team of the Glasgow Training Corps (Caledonian Railway Section) visited Strathaven and engaged in a shooting match with the team of the local Miniature Rifle Club at the range of the latter in Newton Road. The first match was local lady members- v- visiting gentlemen - four-a-side. This resulted in a win for the visitors by 6 points, the scores being - Glasgow, 104, Strathaven, 98. Miss Mary Hamilton was top scorer of the match. Thereafter the two teams contended - nine-a-side, and on this occasion victory rested with Strathaven by 24 points. Totals:- Glasgow, 229 ; Strathaven, 253. The company then adjourned to the Buck's Head Hotel, where a fine supper was served in Mrs Hamilton's well-known style. Rev. John Muirhead gave a racy address on the necessity for every citizen being able to handle a rifle at the present time. He also congratulated the visitors on their good shooting. Mr Wright suitably replied, after which the remainder of the evening was pleasantly spent in harmony and dancing.

Flower Service:

The annual flower service of the East U.F. Church Sabbath School took place on Sunday evening last. The church was elaborately and gracefully decorated by the Sabbath School teachers with flowers and plants, kindly supplied by members of the congregation. At the Sabbath School children on entering made a flower offering, the flower gifts being afterwards sent to the Cowcaddens district of Glasgow. The Rev. Matthew Urie Baird, M.S., minister of the congregation, gave an appropriate and interesting address to the children. He took as his subject "My Garden." reminding them that they had each a garden to keep in order even the garden of the heart and advising them to tend it well so that only sweet and fragrant flowers might grow there - the flowers of purity, truth and love. The choir sang an anthem - "Oh Lord how Manifold," and Mr Mitchell, Union Bank House, two solos,

"Angels ever bright and fair" and "The Better Land," all of which were much appreciated. The church was filled to its utmost capacity, and the collection amounted to £7.5s, which goes to the benefit of the Sabbath School funds.

Death of Strathaven Native in Canada:

The following appears in the "Grandview Exponent," Grandview, Manitoba, of the 5th ult:- *"The home of Charles L. Duncan of Mountain Gap district was stricken down with sorrow last Sunday, August 1st, when the death took place of his beloved wife, Janet Meikle, at the age of 30 years. It was only a little over a week ago that a daughter was born to Mr and Mrs Duncan, and Mrs Duncan was thought to be progressing favourably when complications set in which resulted in her death on the above date. Deceased was born at High Dyke, Strathaven, Lanarkshire, Scotland, and came to Canada about two years ago to be married. Wm. Meikle, of Turleford, Sask., brother of deceased, arrived too late to see his sister in life, but was in time for the funeral, which took place at Grandview Cemetery on Monday, August 2nd. Rev. H. Dickson officiated at the funeral, assisted by Rev. R. J. C. Campbell and G. Mitchell. The late Mrs Duncan was well-known and respected by many people in this district and much sympathy is felt for Mr Duncan in his sad bereavement."* Mrs Duncan before leaving Scotland was a highly accomplished butter maker and attended the large shows with much success as a competitor both in Scotland and England. Her accomplishments were highly esteemed in the land of her adoption.

Issue: Saturday, 11th September, 1915.

Best Kept Station:

The Caledonian Railway Company have issued their awards for 1915. Strathaven Central Station has been awarded a second-class prize of £4, with 94 points (6 from possible). We congratulate Mr Thorburn and his staff, and hope they will be able to go "one better" next year.

Issue: Saturday, 25th September, 1915.

Cheery Hello from the Dardanelles -

Strathaven Callan's Optimistic Hope:

"I'm in the best of health and still going strong. The very day I set foot on the Peninsula I had my first experience of shell fire. We had only been landed about half an hour when the Turks started to shell us, and I can tell you I thought I was in for a rough time of it. However, we were not long in digging ourselves in, and then we felt a bit safer. We get plenty of hard work out here, and pretty dangerous work sometimes, such as digging trenches in the open with bullets flying all around. There is hardly a time we go out but some of the boys get wounded. You may think it strange, but we get quite used to it and never bother, but I can tell you it makes us work to get a little cover. We get bathing in the sea every day when out of the trenches, but we have to stick eight days in them at a time, without a wash, so you can guess we get a bit dirty. The dust lies about six inches on the main roads and about three inches elsewhere. The heat is terrible and when we are marching the dust gets into our boots, so you can guess what our feet are like. I am continually washing socks. But the worst of the lot is the flies. It doesn't matter where I go, there are about a thousand of the pests round about me. I can hardly get taking my food for them - in fact, between flies and dust, I have quite a feed sometimes. Well, to look on the other side, the food is pretty good. We get fresh bread every day. We also have concerts now and again, but unlike our comrades in France we have to supply the "star" turns ourselves, but they are always a huge success. The officers attend and also help to swell the programme, and I can tell you we have the best of talent out here. We hope to be holding a big concert when this is finished, and I don't think it will be extra long now before Johnnie Turk throws

*up his hand. They have made a good stand, and it has been no easy job to put them back to where they are. The Turks are good fighters, and their snipers do a lot of mischief, They are crack shots with the rifle and men not to be played with; but of course, they are no match for the boys of the bull dog breed. If some of the young men were out here they would see that they are needed to give us a hand. We are all quite happy and cheerful, and it is the general opinion that we will be home before Christmas. As for myself! I expect to spend Ne'erday in auld Stra'ven. Yours faithfully **A.B. John R. Malone.***

Issue: Saturday, 2nd October, 1915.

Select Choir:

The attention of those who are musically inclined is called to advertisement of the opening of select choir session on Tuesday. Mr Baxter will again be in charge, and it is hoped there will be a good attendance.

War Fund Kinderspiel:

Attention is directed to advertisement regarding the above. The kinderspiel to be produced this winter will be the popular one entitled "Princess Chrysenthemum." Mr John D. Findlay is convener, and Mr James P. Morrison secretary - and their connection with such a worthy object should ensure a great success.

Autumn Holiday:

There was a large crowd of visitors in the town on Monday in connection with the Glasgow autumn holiday. The weather was brilliant, and the trippers were thus in a position to make the very best of the day's outing. The 6.45 p.m. train had to be duplicated, and the 9.50 which had several extra coaches was absolutely packed. The holiday was observed in all the local works.

Strathaven and the War:

Corporal Thomas McColl Weir, (formerly in Messrs Gebbie & Wilson's office) 1st Battalion London Scottish, in First Brigade with Black Watch and Camerons, etc., was wounded last Saturday, during the attack. He had a bullet wound in the left elbow, and was weakened by loss of blood before being picked up in the open. He was sent down to base hospital in France and is progressing satisfactorily.

The Banflatts Burglary:

Robert Wilson, labourer, who was arrested in connection with the recent house-breaking at Banflatts Farm, appeared before Lord Cullen in the High Court at Edinburgh on Wednesday. The charge preferred against him was that of stealing two gold brooches, a gold neck chain, and other articles of jewellery and 2s 6d. Counsel for the defence said there was nothing to advance in favour of his client, except that at the time he was under the influence of drink. Lord Cullen said the prisoner apparently had a long criminal career, although the longest sentence he had received was one of twelve months imprisonment. The sentence now was three years' penal servitude.

The Pictures:

A high standard of pictures continues to be maintained at the Picture House, every film vying with another for premier place from a "popularity" point of view. Some excitement was caused among the youngsters by the star picture of Saturday, "In the Days of Thundering Herd," introducing, as it did, the ever popular cowboys and Red Indians. "The Master Key," which has now reached the fifth episode, maintains its popularity, whilst Mr Main's selection of comics are screamers every time. At very considerable expense it has been arranged to introduce the powerful serial drama "The Black Box." As will be seen from advertisement, this sensational piece commenced on Monday first, and will be shown Monday and Tuesday of each week for fifteen weeks.

Strathaven and the War:

Lance Corporal John Hood, writing from Woolwich Hospital on Wednesday, gives an interesting account of the British forward move last Saturday. With his battalion, the 5th Royal Highlanders, he was in a charge on the German trenches, and practically at the end of the assault he was struck on the cheek by a bullet, which penetrated his mouth and removed some teeth. The doctor does not consider his condition serious and even states that his face will not be badly marked. We are pleased to be able to state that the rumour regarding the death of Private Somers, R.F.A., is unfounded. It gained currency in the following way:- Pte. Somers had written a letter to his wife whilst on the field, and was unable to post it at the time. Later he lost the letter, which was picked up by a soldier and sent on with an explanatory note. Mrs Somers has since received a letter of later date in which he states that he is well. - Private James A. Carruthers, 6th Scottish Rifles, was posted as missing after the charge of his battalion at Festubert on 15th June, and since that date no further information has been received by his parents. Should this paragraph meet the eye of any of the 6th who can give information, the same will be most welcome. The address is 23 Townhead Street, Strathaven.

Strathaven and War Economy:

"Sir, We are having put forth on every hand the importance of economy being practised by all grades of society, and in view of the existing circumstances, rightly so. Yet we see the principles being discarded in various circles and ways, from the Government to local bodies and committees - notably the Belgian Relief Committee in our town. I believe I voice the sentiments of not a few when I state that the expense incurred by the issue in book term of their report on the amount lately collected by public subscription for the relief of the Belgians in our midst, and otherwise, might have been saved and put to the fund for the further amelioration of the distress caused by the lamentable war. The total amount published in the local paper should have been sufficient to satisfy the curiosity of any patriotic subscriber. The first, I am sure, were not given for the sake of publicity. Trusting the hint given may be taken by those responsible for any future subscription lists." A Sympathetic Subscriber.

Issue: Saturday, 9th October, 1915.

Care of the Wounded:

On Friday evening last there was a good attendance in the Public Hall to hear a lecture by Miss E.M.C. Fogge of Glasgow on the Scottish Women's Hospitals in France and Serbia. His Grace the Duke of Hamilton presided.

Issue: Saturday, 16th October, 1915.

Accident:

On Wednesday evening a little girl named Nessie Anderson of Castle Terrace was knocked down and run over by a motor cycle entering the locus from the Stonehouse Road. She was carried into Ms Cochran's shop in Main Street, but she soon revived and was able to proceed home with some support.

Strathaven and the War:

The following reports have been received during the week:-

Official intimation has been received of the death of Alexander Watson, Royal Scots, killed in action on 27th September. Before enlisting Pte. Watson was employed as a tailor in the town. He was married and leaves a widow and two young children.

Intimation has also been received that about the same date, Pte. William Mitchell, Cameron Highlanders, was killed. The parents of Pte. Mitchell reside at Hookhead Cottage. The lad served his apprenticeship as a blacksmith at Caldermill, and was subsequently employed in Motherwell.

Conflicting reports continue to arrive suggesting Pte. Thomas Knowles, Argyll and Sutherland Highlanders, is a casualty, but as none of them are official his friends are hoping for the best.

Pte. John Aiton, Royal Highlanders, whose mother resides at Ballgreen, was wounded in the hand and "gassed" in the big advance. He is now sufficiently recovered to be able to write home himself.

Pte. George Muir, 2 Castle Street, Royal Field Artillery, has been wounded on the knee in action in the Dardanelles, and is making good progress in hospital.

Leading Seaman Thomas Stewart, Royal Naval Division is in hospital ill. He is with the Dardanelles forces also. His home address is Todshill Street.

Pte. William Semple, 11 Lethame Road, who is with the Australian Field Force in the Dardanelles, has been wounded on head and neck.

Pte. John McMath, Royal Highlanders, has been wounded in France. His parents reside at Westlinbank.

Pte. Matthew Thorburn, Station House, who is with the Royal Highlanders, is in hospital at Aldershot, having been wounded on the knee at Loos on 28th September. He is doing well, and has been visited by several Strathaven men who are stationed at Aldershot

Issue: Saturday, 23rd October, 1915.

University Success:

Miss Annie B. Henderson, Bank of Scotland House, has passed the final examination for the degree of B.Sc., Glasgow University. Miss Henderson is probably the first lady student from Strathaven who has obtained this important degree in science.

Issue: Saturday, 30th October, 1915.

Sudden Death:

On Sunday a young woman named Maggie Ross employed as a domestic servant at Willowbank died suddenly. She was quite her usual on Saturday, but on Sunday she complained of feeling ill and expressed the desire to be sent home. Arrangements were made to have this carried out, and a motor car was ordered, but whilst the preparations were in progress the girl died. The body was conveyed to the home of her parents at Bothwell. - On Thursday a well-known townsman, Mr William Prentice, died very suddenly. Mr Prentice was at his work in the smithy as usual on Thursday morning, and at the breakfast hour he became ill and expired almost immediately. Deceased had been in the doctor's care for some time, but nothing serious was anticipated. Mr Prentice came to Strathaven over thirty years ago, and was employed by Mr William Miller, Townhead Street. After a time an opening occurred at Caldermill and he started there on his own account. His business developing more on the east side of Caldermill, Mr Prentice had a smithy built in Strathaven, and here he has been for a number of years. Mr Prentice was a quiet, steady dependable man, very popular with the class amongst whom he found his work. He took no part in public matters, but was a leading member of the Gospel Hall. He leaves a widow and grown-up family for whom much sympathy is felt.

Recruiting Meeting;

A public meeting was held on Tuesday in the Lesser Hall, the hall being crowded. Mr James Cameron, C.C., was appointed chairman, and invited expressions of opinion. Mr James Barrie moved that the meeting pledge itself to give all support to Lord Derby's appeal. Mr J. S. Napier seconded, and the motion was unanimously adopted. Each one seemed to realise the urgent necessity for every fit man to coming forward and enlisting himself now. A large representative recruiting committee was formed, with Mr Cameron, convener; Mr J S Duncan, recruiting officer; and Mr A. Wilson, secretary. Mr Duncan gave details of the suggestions and instructions for the personal canvass, and intimated that recruits could be attested at the Parish Council Office during office hours, and from 6 to 8 p.m. daily (including Saturdays). A good number of those present undertook to act as canvassers under Lord Derby's scheme.

Issue: Saturday, 13th November, 1915.

Local Soldiers:

We had a short visit during the week from Driver Claude Barrie, R.F.A., Claude was a bombardier in India when war broke out, and gave up his stripes to come over with another Battery. He has had many narrow escapes, but so far is uninjured. Claude looks "as hard as nails, and as fit as a fiddle." - Lance Sergeant Thomas Stewart, R.N. Division, is now recovering from his illness, and is back at duty in the Dardanelles.

Sad Death of a Native:

Our readers will learn with regret of the death of Mr John S. Alston, 11 McNeill Street, Larkhall, a son of the late Thomas Alston, town postman. Mr Alston met with an accident at his work fully three weeks ago, falling from a height on to some railings which impaled him. So great was the loss of blood at the time that the doctor had little hope for him, but for three weeks he rallied slightly. Then on Monday it was considered advisable to remove him to the Royal Infirmary, Glasgow. In the course of the journey Mr Alston died in High Street. A pathetic coincidence attaches to the occurrence in that it was practically at the same place, at the same hour of the day that his well-known brother, Mr James H. Alston died a year and eight months ago, and both corpses were carried into the same place. Much sympathy is felt for Mrs Alston and family.

Issue: Saturday, 20th November, 1915.

Honour to Strathaven Officer:

Strathaven learned with pride on Saturday, that the French Legion of Honour had been conferred on Captain James Lusk, Dunavon, for conspicuous bravery along the advance of the 6th Scottish Rifles at Festubert in June.

Our Soldiers:

Pte. John Aiton, Royal Highlanders arrived home at the end of last week, having been discharged hospital. John has had the misfortune to lose an eye, but accepts his fate with his usual cheerful optimism. Pte. James Paterson, Southend, of the same battalion, is on seven days' leave. He went through the recent big advance unscathed. James tells that as they were charging across the open towards the German trenches he heard a voice shouting *"go on, Stra'ven."* and, looking along, he got a glimpse of Sandy McKenzie, (Commercial Road), who was in another battalion advancing simultaneously with him. Pte. Matthew Thorburn has so far recovered from his injury to be allowed home. He is still pretty lame, and has to get along with the help of a stick. There was a regular Black Watch gathering in Commercial Road on Tuesday when Matthew took unto himself a wife. The bride is Miss Catherine Steel. - Pte. John Russell, North Street, is also home on leave. All of these lads belong to the Royal Highlanders. - A letter from Leading Seaman Thomas Stewart indicates that he has not returned to duty as we intimated last Saturday, but that he has been sent to this country for treatment. He is presently in Charing Cross Hospital, London.

Fatal Accident:

On Sunday last, when the churches were coming out at one o'clock, an old man named Hugh McLelland, 76 years of age was on his way home from the East United Free Church to Thomson Street, when he was knocked down by the side-car of a motor cycle. Dr. Alan Watt was quickly in attendance, and certified that the man's skull had been fractured, and directed that he should be removed to the Infirmary in Glasgow. On the way to the Infirmary McLelland died at Cadzow.

Issue: Saturday, 4th December, 1915.

Killed in Action:

Information has reached Mr James Muldoon, Priestgill Farm, Strathaven, that his second son, Andrew, has been killed in action in France on 8th November. The deceased lad was 20 years of age, and previous to his enlistment in February into the 5th Batt. Cameron Highlanders, was employed as ploughman at Brackenridge Farm. When resident in East Kilbride parish Private Muldoon gained some fame as a quoiter in the Auldhouse Club. He was only a few months married. An older brother, James is at the front with the 2nd Battalion of the same regiment, and so far has escaped injury.

Issue: Saturday, 11th December, 1915.

Local Soldiers:

Lieutenant and Quartermaster Jennings of the 14th Royal Scots, has been promoted Hon Captain.

Lance-Corporal Thomas M. Weir, London Scottish, has been granted a commission as Second Lieutenant and transferred to the Argyll and Sutherland Highlanders. He is quite recovered from his wound and looking in better health than ever. Sergt. James Anderson, Canadian Highlanders, favoured us with a call on Saturday prior to returning to the front. James's wound was on the upper arm and is now quite better. The following interesting letter from Pte. William Craig, 7th Seaforth Highlanders, throws some light on the fate of his cousin, Pte. William Howitt, whose death in action we reported some time ago, but which was afterwards regarded as uncertain:-

"Just a few lines to let you know that I am still well, hoping all at home are the same. I am in the trenches at present, but am going back shortly for a rest. The other day I met a chap who came to us from the 2nd Batt. Seaforths, and on asking him if he knew Willie Howitt, this is what he told me, and as this all happened some months ago I don't think I'm doing anything wrong in writing you about

it:- The Seaforths, with the Dublin Fusiliers on the left and the Royal Warwicks on the right, were making an attack on St Julian Wood, and, being a lot of men the Royal Warwicks began to get separated from the Seaforths, leaving a gap. Willie brought up his machine gun to cover this gap (Willie was the No. 1 eg gunner and was in charge of gun and gun team). They saw the German cavalry forming up preparing to charge. Willie, setting his sight, on them, began firing, and Lance-Corporal Vickery, who was telling me this, says it was the best thing that he had ever seen done as he lay and watched Willie firing and sniping the saddles empty, without so much as touching one of the horses. He went on to say that the whole gun team were to be recommended for the V.C., but unhappily a shell exploded right above the gun killing the team and annihilating the gun, (Lance-Corporal Vickery was wounded shortly after). Willie was killed outright and did not suffer any. There is at least some little consolation in that. I am sure you will feel very proud of Willie when you read this. You will be glad that he did his bit, and you won't be sorry that I am trying to do mine.

Issue: Saturday, 25th December, 1915.

The Late Dr. Dan Dougal:

The many friends of the late D. Daniel Dougal will be interested to read the following reference by the Rev. J. D. Jones, D.D., in the "Richmond Hill Magazine and Congregational Record"; also a reference by Rev. Alexander Corbett in the "Lansdowne Baptist Magazine:"

"Since I wrote the notes of last month's Magazine, we have lost Dr Dougal from our fellowship.

Dr. Dougal, before he came to us, had been the doctor of a Scottish country parish. In his devotion to his medical duties, oftentimes - travelling miles on horseback in bitter wintry weather, he had to endure a great deal of hardship, and the hardships so endured left their mark upon him. But I never looked at his hands - knotted as they were with rheumatism without feeling that they were like a soldier's wounds, the marks of an honourable and devoted service. He came down to Bournemouth some years ago to spend the evening of his years, and he and Mrs Dougal attached themselves to our church. In all sorts of quiet ways the Doctor helped forward the work of the church. He responded to all the appeals made from the pulpit, and was especially kind in cases of need and distress. I ventured on many an occasion to ask him to visit some of our sick poor. He did so gladly, putting his medical skill at their disposal, and something besides medical skill as well. He was Scotch in his reserve, but more than once he and I talked frankly about the deepest things, and his whole trust was in his Lord. He passed peacefully away on October 25th, after months of weakness bravely and patiently borne."

"I record with sorrow the death of my friend, Dr. Dougal. He was a member at Richmond Hill, but in late years he often worshipped with us at Lansdowne as it was nearer to him than his own church. When his health permitted him to do so, he gave e both time and skill to the help of the needy, and many will miss his kindly and helpful presence. He had a long and lingering illness, which he bore with unmurmuring fortitude."

Hamilton Advertiser

Issue: Saturday, 1st January, 1916.

Postal Notice:

On New Year's Day there will only be one delivery in the morning and one dispatch at 2.40 pm. The office will be open as on Sunday's from 9 till 10 am for telegraphs.

Dramatic Entertainment:

A meeting called by advert, of all willing to assist in a proposed dramatic entertainment in favour of Red Cross Funds was held in the Public Hall on Monday evening. There was an encouraging attendance and it was unanimously decided to proceed with the project. After some consideration "Rob Roy" was decided on as the piece to be produced. See advert.

Parish Council of Avondale:

A meeting was held on Tuesday. Present: Messrs Andrew Barr, D.B. Black, R.B.. Galloway, John Hamilton, John Wiseman, Wm. Wright and Wm. Dykes (Chairman). A number of appeals against payment of County Council and Parish Council rates were decided - Mr. Cameron, C.C., attending during the consideration of these cases. Business in connection with Poor Law and finance was taken up, and the council agreed not to meet in January.

The Pictures:

Last Saturday evening's programme was probably the most interesting ever presented in Strathaven. The beautiful three-part drama - "Her Supreme Sacrifice" - was immensely enjoyed. It was full of tender pathos, which touched the audience as few subjects do, especially when the heroine finally deserted the wealth and luxury with which she was surrounded to go back to her now crippled first lover. Throughout the week the variety of the programme has been marvellous. During the holiday week very special attractions are advertised.

Christmas Services:

A special service was conducted in the Parish Church on Sunday evening, when several carols and anthems were beautifully rendered by the choir, under the conductorship of Mr William Ferguson - Misses Watson (contralto) and Miller (soprano) did well in their solos. Rev. John Muirhead, B.D., presided and preached an appropriate sermon. In the East United Free Church special musical items were introduced and well rendered by the choir, Mr David Hamilton leading. The soloists were Forenoon : Mr A.C. Hilston, Jnr. - Evening - Misses Frances Brown & Annie Tennent. All acquitted themselves well. Rev. Matthew Urie Baird preached at both diets.

A Brave Cameron:

Mrs Hendry, 189 Bellfield Street, Dennistoun, Glasgow, has received the following letter announcing that her son, Alexander, who unfortunately died on 10th May, had been mentioned in dispatches - *"War Office, November 29, 1915 - Madam, I have it in command from His Majesty the King to inform you that your son, the late Private Alex Hendry (9377) 2nd Cameron Highlanders, was mentioned in a dispatch from Field-Marshall Sir John French, dated May 31st, 1915 and published in the "London Gazette" dated June 22nd, for gallant and distinguished service in the field. His Majesty desires to condole with you on the loss you have sustained and to express his high appreciation of the service of the late Alexander Hendry. - I have the honour to be your obedient servant, Lieutenant-Colonel, Assistant Military Secretary."*

Red Cross Work Party:

Mrs H. Lee Dykes desires to express her thanks for the following very acceptable donations to the funds of the Red Cross Party - surplus from Avondale Farmers' Society Show, 1915, per Mr Mitchell, Union Bank, Hon Treas, £50.5s.6d; surplus from Lodge "St. Andrew", No. 215 Strathaven, concert, per Mr Robert Thomson, Treas, £4.1s.8d; proceeds of Barnock Whist Drive, per Miss Holmes, £10. Mrs Lee Dykes despatched on December 18th to the Matron, No.5 General Hospital,

Rouen - 3 shirts, 18 amputation bags, 3 pairs operating stockings, 10 pairs socks, 3 bed jackets, 3 pairs pants, 6 vests, 12 milk bowl covers, 6 mufflers, 6 pockets and 2 body belts. On December 30th - to the Matron, No.8 General Hospital, Rouen - 4 shirts, 4 fever shirts, 20 pairs socks, 18 amputation bags, 12 milk bowl covers, 2 bed jackets, 4 vests, 2 pairs operating stockings, 18 pockets, 5 pairs cuffs, and 12 mufflers. A parcel of comforts was received from the Parish Church Needlework Guild and was forwarded to Mrs Daly, Princes Gardens, Glasgow for the 6th Highland Light Infantry, now at Dardanelles.

Entertainment at Dungavel:

The Duke and Duchess of Hamilton gave a Christmas treat to the children of Barnock School on Saturday last at 3 o'clock. The company also included their Graces and the household. Prior to the dismantling of the Christmas tree, a charming little entertainment was given by the ducal children. Lady Jean, Lady Margaret, the Marquis of Douglas and Clydesdale, Lord George and Lord Malcolm - consisting of songs, recitations and a sketch from "Alice in Wonderland". They all acquitted themselves splendidly, and evoked rounds of applause from the audience. "Father Christmas" appeared at the close of the sketch and addressed the children in a jovial way, saying he felt very fit and well, but he rather disliked the cut of his whiskers because they were too much like those of old Von Tirpitz. Tirpitz, he was glad to say was suffering from cold feet in the Kiel Canal, where things were a bit crowded, but he rather thought "cold feet" in Kiel was preferable to "hot water" in the North Sea. "Father Christmas" then produced a gift for each guest present, including some Belgian refugees in the neighbourhood. The proceedings concluded with 3 ringing cheers for the Duke and Duchess and family, and one cheer more for "Father Christmas" whose role was played by Mr T.B. Hotte. The company was afterwards entertained to tea.

Issue: Saturday, 8th January, 1916.

Postal Notice:

Owing to the change of departure of the train at 6.40 p.m., the letter box will now be closed at 6.15 p.m.

The Pictures:

Mr Main's Ne'erday arrangements proved very acceptable and large houses were obtained at the watch-night and week-end performances. The programmes were really "class". In the coming week "The Exploits of Elaine" take first place in point of interest, while the "Black Box" runs to a finish. Fine variety is announced in the week's arrangements.

School Board:

The usual monthly meeting of the Board was held in the Board Room on Tuesday. Dr. Mason,

Chairman of the Board presided. Several applications for exemption were dealt with, most of which were refused. Attention is drawn to the advertisement of a lecture to be given on "Food Production in War Time" by a County Council lecturer in Crosshill School on Tuesday evening. The Clerk submitted the annual accounts of the Young's Bequest which, after being gone over, were remitted to the auditor.

B.W.T.A:

The mothers' meeting in connection with the British Women's Temperance Association was held in the Good Templars' Hall on Wednesday afternoon. There was a splendid turnout. In the absence of

Mrs Lusk, president, Mrs Dey opened the meeting. After tea, Mrs Fischer, Larkhall, gave a most inspiring address. Miss Muir sang two solos, accompanied by Miss Bryson. The Messrs Bryson and Miss Bryson gave a fine dialogue, also recitations. Altogether the meeting was enjoyable. At the close a few pledges were taken for the Cradle Roll.

Soup Kitchen:

The claims on this popular institution are, during the present winter, proving more numerous than usual, the attendance of children each day averaging about 100. The festive season, however, has not passed without bringing its customary treat to these children in the way of special fare. Mr Murray of Stromelloch has generously continued his gift of a sheep, which was distributed on Friday of last week in the form of pies. Gifts of fruit and sweets for each child have also been very kindly presented by Mr and Mrs Baird, Gilholm.

Issue: Saturday, 15th January, 1916,

Evangelistic:

Mr W. W. Faraday of Bakewell, one of the foremost evangelists of the day, has been conducting meetings in the Gospel Hall. His subjects and the unusual style of his addresses have interested and instructed the large audiences which assembled nightly to hear him.

Mentioned in Dispatches:

Nurse J Walker of Green Street, attached to the Civil Hospital Reserve, has been mentioned in dispatches by Sir John French and recommended by him for gallant and distinguished service. Nurse Walker was trained for 3 years in Kilmarnock Infirmary after having had previous former experience. She was appointed Theatre Sister in 1912, and in 1914 Surgical Ward Sister. She was called up for service in November, 1914 and has been in active service ever since, with the exception of a short furlough at the end of last year - Quartermaster and Hon. Lieutenant John Donald, of the 3rd Dragoon Guards, has also been mentioned in Sir John French's dispatches for devotion to duty and gallantry in the field. Lieutenant Donald is the eldest son of Mr William Donald, farmer, Hairshawhead. He has been 16 years in the Regular Army and has risen from the ranks. We heartily congratulate Nurse Walker and Lieutenant Donald on this signal mark of honour.

Died in Hospital:

We regret to announce the death in Murdos Hospital of our young townsman, Private William Brownlie, 1st Royal Scots, second son of Mr William Brownlie, Bridge Street. Private Brownlie has seen a considerable amount of soldiering. Commencing with the Volunteers he served for a time in the old "K" Company, 2nd V.B.S.R., in which his father also served for over 20 years, then he joined the 2nd Battalion of the Cameron Highlanders shortly after that battalion was formed. Being invalided from the Cameron's he soon regained his health and then threw in his lot with the Scottish Rifles, with which corps he soldiered in India. On the outbreak of the present war Private Brownlie joined the Highland Light Infantry with which he went to the front. He was wounded in the thigh, and after being discharged from hospital was transferred to the 1st Battalion Royal Scots with which regiment he saw service in the Mediterranean. During the latter period he contracted the illness from which he died.

Issue: Saturday, 22nd January, 1916.

Gilmourton MIA:

The meeting on Wednesday night was very well attended by both ladies and gentlemen. The chairman was Mr Archd. Hamilton, and the speaker was Mr Walter Weir who gave a very fine lecture on "Robert Burns". It was a splendid address and everyone there felt proud that night that Burns was a Scotsman. Mr Weir also favoured the company with a comic reading which was much appreciated.

War Relief:

The committee met on Tuesday night - Mr W Sym, J,P., C.C., in the chair. It was estimated that the income from the flag day and donations amounted to £35.6s.3d. Expenses for postages and parcels etc., £34.16s.10d leaving a balance of 9s.5d. It was intimated that 190 parcels were sent to local persons at Christmas and that 72 tons of coal had been distributed to the dependents of soldiers in the village. The committee are greatly indebted to the contractors and farmers who gratuitously did the carting and also to the gentlemen who supported the distribution. It was agreed to authorise the Fund Committee to deal with any case requiring temporary relief.

Our Soldier Lads:

We have a short but cheery note this week from R.A. Fleming, of the Army Pay Corps who is "Somewhere in France". We note with pleasure that he has now attained the rank of Sergeant. Good Luck! There's higher rungs yet Bob! Another of our correspondents is Private Robert Hill who is also "over there" with one of the service battalions of the Cameronians. He has already seen a lot of fighting and, so far, has escaped unscathed. Private Hiss is another of the old members of "K" Company, 2nd V.B.S.R., which at one time flourished here. Sergeant Wm. Cochrane, North Street, of the Royal Garrison Artillery, is presently on short furlough from the front. He is suffering a little with his legs, but it is expected that a little attention will get him fit as a fiddle again. William mobilised all the way from Australia. One of the young Owens in a letter home from the "near east" tells of meeting Willie Giffen, who is now a Company Sergeant Major, in the Royal Engineers. Giffen was one of the first recruits of the 2nd Battalion of the Cameron Highlanders when it was raised, and saw service in Egypt, being present at the battle of Omdurman. Afterwards he served in the Royal Engineers. He was "clear" of the army when the war broke out but the old spirit was there and he re-enlisted. He is the elder brother of Lt. James Giffen, Cameron Highlanders who we are sorry to hear has been badly wounded on the leg.

Issue: Saturday, 12th February, 1916.

Warning:

Persons receiving 10s Treasury Notes would do well to carefully examine them, as a counterfeit was passed in a shop here last week. On the false note the word "Ten Shillings" are in rather clumsy type and the King's head is not good.

Production of a New Scottish opera - "The Shade of Burns".

Dr Robert Machardy is a strong champion of Scottish music. He claims our national melodies to be the most beautiful in the world with the true inherent power to entertain and charm the most artistic temperaments. His enthusiasm in this direction amounts almost to an obsession, and he is wont in season and out of season to demonstrate the great possibilities of our Scottish song. To his many musical arrangements and compositions, including the "Prince Charlie" grand opera, he has added a

Scottish opera, which, in homage to our immortal bard, he has entitled "The Shade of Burns." It is dedicated to Lord Newlands, and has been graciously accepted by His Majesty the King. Dr. Machardy is responsible for both libretto and music. Briefly, the scheme of the opera is that, following upon the singing of a grand Scottish chorus with orchestra and bagpipes, Burns returns to earth to express his love of his native land and its national music. The scene of the visit is the banks of the Lugar, where the poet meets with Lady Scotia Doon, with whom Lord Lugar is in love. The other characters introduced are Beneva, the daughter of a Highland chieftain, and a jester, who, as a satirist, gives his opinion on love, music, opera, the neglect of genius in life, and the posthumous honours heaped upon it when too late. The Opera was produced in the Public Hall, Strathaven, on Thursday evening, when a fairly large and representative audience was presided over by Dr. Mason. It would not be correct to say the performance was an unqualified success, but, making due allowance for a certain crudeness in a first production, the lack of a fully equipped orchestra, and the many embarrassing circumstances that Dr Machardy has had to overcome since the rehearsals started, the opera on the whole was given a fair interpretation, and was received with general favour by the audience. It was noticeable, however, that a section of the audience, from their boisterous exuberance and hilarity, were not inclined to consider the opera seriously, and in this respect Dr. Machardy was but suffering what the chairman hinted at in his opening remarks, the penalty of the prophet who is not honoured in his own country. The music of the opera is bold and vigorous in tone, and there are many passages reflecting a wonderful range of harmonic colour, the full effect of which could only be obtained by a complete orchestral accompaniment. The "book" also is meritorious, some of the stanzas, indeed, reaching a very high level. In the production of the opera, the title role was adopted by Mr James Stewart, who in general get-up was a splendid character and might have posed for the poet himself. His singing was well received. Miss M. Allan, L. Mus, was a delightful "Lady Scotia," and her cultured singing was a feature of the performance. She was ably seconded as a vocalist by Miss Watson, in the character of "Beneva." Both ladies were frequently loudly applauded. As "Lord Lugar," Mr Hugh Macdonald gave a quiet, yet fairly effective interpretation of the part. Dr Machardy was the "Jester," and he also was fairly successful, though he excels as a musician rather than as a vocalist. Valuable services were rendered the production by Miss Dempster, pianist, and Messrs C Kyle and D. Forbes. Violinists. They contributed the various accompaniments with much ability and intelligence. We believe it is Dr. Zachary's intention to produce the opera shortly in Glasgow under more promising auspices as to orchestra etc.

Issue: Saturday. 19th February, 1916.

Property Market:

On Tuesday last there was exposed to public sale within the Public Hall, 'Vicarlea Cottage', Townhead Street, at the upset price of £450. After keen competition, the property was sold to Mr Walter Elder, manufacturer, at the price of £500. The Strathaven Auction Mart (Ltd) were the auctioneers, while the agent was Mr J. McFarlane Paterson, writer.

Issue: Saturday, 26th February, 1916.

Mutual Improvement Association:

"The Autobiography of Dr. Alexander Carlyle" was the subject of a lecture delivered last Monday evening by the Rev. John Muirhead, B.D..

Issue: Saturday, 4th March, 1916.

Master Blacksmiths Meet:

A meeting of the Master Blacksmiths of the town and surrounding parishes was held in Strathaven on Saturday evening - Mr William Hamilton, J.P., Chapelton, presiding. In view of the serious increase in the price of material etc., caused by the war, it was unanimously decided to increase the price of jobbing of all descriptions, and a new tariff was drawn up.

Fire:

An outbreak of fire resulting in the total destruction of the building occurred at the Good Templar Hall, Ward Street, on Tuesday morning. The first indication of anything being wrong was at 4 o'clock when some people living opposite were awakened by the glare of the flames. By this time the fire had got such a strong hold that the roof had commenced to collapse. The fire brigade, under Sergeant McMurdo, was summoned and were speedily on the spot, but the task set them was a hopeless one, and as indicated the building, became a total wreck. The Good Templar Hall was a timber erection and was only opened at Christmas 1908. In addition to being a place of meeting for "Drumclog" Lodge, No.211 I.O.G.T. the proprietors, it was open regularly as a Recreation Room and was utilised by the B.W.T.A. for mothers' meetings, was the regular meeting place of the Christadelphians, and was granted annually for the use of the Soup Kitchen Committee. All the regalia of the lodge was destroyed, and the total loss, which is covered by insurance, is about £400.

Issue: Saturday, 11th March, 1916.

Fire:

At three o'clock on the morning of Friday last, the local fire brigade was called to an outbreak of fire which had occurred at Glencaple, Kirk Street. It appears that some ignited coal from the fire had got under the hearthstone and set fire to the beams of the upper storey. The brigade got right to the seat of the fire and immediately extinguished it before much damage was done.

Lighting Restriction:

Compliance with the Order issued by the Chief Constable of Lanarkshire has been pretty complete here, in fact there has been considerably more obscuring of lights than subduing. There is just one point to which a little attention might be given, viz., in cases where the window blinds are narrow it would be advisable to affix strips of darkening material, either to the blind or the sides of the window.

Issue: Saturday, 18th March, 1916.

Sudden Death:

Much regret has been caused by the sudden death of Mr Vallance Stewart, junior partner of the firm of Messrs. Stewart Bros, fleshers, Commongreen, which took place in Glasgow in the early hours of last Saturday morning. On the previous day Mr Stewart had been on his way to Kilmarnock with his brother when he took suddenly ill. He was immediately brought home, and on the advice of the doctor sent to Glasgow to undergo an operation. He endured great agony, and, as stated, died in the early hours of Saturday. A man of cheery, happy-go-lucky disposition, he was extremely popular with the large number of people with whom he did business, and his death at the early age of thirty-nine is much regretted. He leaves a widow and a young family of seven.

Who's Who in Passaic County - A Stra'ven Callan in the States:

The following notice of a Strathaven man appears in a recent issue of "Hart's Counsellor and Critique":- *"William H. Young, Counsellor at Law, and Judge of the Police Court of the City of Paterson, and a general all-round good fellow, is a shining example of a self-made man. Raised to his present position by the dint of his own labours, Mr Young's career speaks volumes for the possibilities that await the young man of today. William H. Young was born in Strathaven, Lanarkshire, Scotland, on April 1868, and came to this city thirty-six years ago. He has resided all that time in the City of Paterson, entered the employ of James Rogers, who then ran a silk mill, and soon became an expert warper. He worked in the silk mill until he decided to take up the study of law and entered the University of New York, where after three years he graduated with honours and passed the New Jersey Bar Examination in the month of November . . . and has since practised law in this city. Mr Young is still a member of the Horizontal Warpers Association, and in their counsel. He is a brother of Ex-Alderman David Young, and resides at No. 325 Ellison Street, with his wife and one son, a boy 17 years old, who is a student at Steven's Institute. He is a member of a number of organisations and is popular in all of them. A staunch Republican, his present appointment was a tribute to his sterling party loyalty. Since taking the office, Mr Young has brought to the Court a ripe experience in dealing with cases that affect the masses. His judgement is sound and conservative. He thoroughly investigates before making a decision. A keen judge of human nature, he has the characteristics of a Scotchman of being right before making a decision. His friends are legion, for the reason that he is always ready and willing to give up his time to hear anyone that may have a complaint or requires assistance of any kind, and he deserves the success that has come to him."*

Issue: Saturday, 8ᵗʰ April, 1916.

Local Soldiers:

We regret to record two deaths this week of local soldiers - Lance-Corporal McKay, a local postman thought not a local man, has died of wounds at the front. He was a Reservist and went up on mobilisation. Early in the war he was wounded, and after being discharged from hospital, spent a few days here before returning to his regiment. The other is William Semple, son of Mr John Semple, Lethame Road, who has died in hospital. He was with the Australian Forces. Some time ago, he was wounded in the head and neck, but he was back again in the firing line when he turned ill. Previous to going to Australia, Semple served his time as a butcher with Mr Watt. Townhead Street.

Obituaries:

We regret to record the sudden death of Mr Andrew C. Downie, architect, which took place on Monday. Mr Downie was quite well up to Friday last, but during the week-end he complained a little, and on Monday passed away. Mr Downie was a native of Hamilton, and came here a considerable number of years ago to take up business. In this he was very successful, his undoubted skill and good taste commending him to many who contemplated building. He was greatly interested in the recent production of "Rob Roy," and acted as stage manager. He leaves a widow and grown-up family. - Another well-known Strathaven man passed away in Glasgow last week, viz., Mr Robert Brown. Some years ago he built and ran the mill at Chapel Road, known as Kilwuddie Mill. Whilst in Strathaven he took a lead in all forms of outdoor sport, particularly fishing, in which he was an expert. Latterly he has been associated with some mill interest in the city. Mrs Brown survives her husband and the family are all doing for themselves.

Issue: Saturday, 15th April, 1916.

Obituary:

Death has been busy in our midst during the week, and several well-known persons have received the call. On Monday Mr Samuel Cassels, ironmonger, Barn Street, who has been ailing for some weeks passed away. Mr Cassels was born in Hamilton, his father being Mr David Cassels, the founder of the well-known grocery firm of D. & J. Cassels, Quarry Street, Hamilton. Orphaned early in life he came to Strathaven and was apprenticed to the blacksmith trade under his uncle, who was in business as a veterinary surgeon and blacksmith. When quite a youth Mr Cassels' uncle also died and he carried on the business till a few years ago when he retired in favour of his son David, devoting his own time to the conduct of his ironmongery store. Deceased was a quiet, backward man, but when people got to know him they realised they had met one of exceptional ability and insight. He was not one of the kind ready to accept everybody's opinion, frequently intercepting with a "naw," and then laying off his own well-founded view. In this, however, his vast fund of pawky humour prevented him from giving offence. He was in his 73rd year, and leaves a widow and grown-up family. - On Tuesday, Mrs Adam Brownlie, widow of Adam Brownlie, weaver, died at the age of 72; and on the same day Mrs Andrew Thomson, widow of Andrew Thomson, grain and cheese merchant, died at Vicarland Place at the ripe old age of 85.

Issue: Saturday, 29th April, 1916.

Strathaven and the War:

The friends of Private James Caruthers (2007), 1/6th Scottish Rifles reported missing at Festubert on 15th June 1915, have now had official word that he was killed on that date. Pte. Carruthers was a native of Strathaven and was 19 years of age. He is the second son of Mr Richard Carruthers, 23 Townhead Street, Strathaven, and was employed by Messrs Colville, Motherwell.

Issue: Saturday, 6th May, 1916.

Supplying liquor after hours:

At Hamilton Sheriff Court on Thursday, Thomas Caird, Spirit Merchant, Commongreen, Strathaven, was convicted of a charge of having in the Royal Inn, Strathaven, on April 22, sold or supplied excisable liquor to three customers after the hour of 9 o'clock p.m. Sheriff Shennan imposed a penalty of £12, or 30 days, while a fine of 30s, or seven days, was imposed on each of the others, who were also convicted of having consumed the liquor.

Issue; Saturday, 20th May, 1916.

Milk Supply:

"Sir, - I notice that in some towns a boycott is taking place on the milk supply. Strathaven has long been famed for good butter, milk, and eggs; but I am afraid this cannot be said of our present supplies. I understand that the month of May is the most prolific month of the year for good milk, but in the face of this the measurement has been curtailed to a considerable extent. We had a boycott on the butter lately; why not, if things don't improve on the milk? I trust consumers will stand up for their rights in this respect. **Pro Bono Publico.***"*

Milk Supply:

"Sir, - I was pleased to see such a timely letter in the "H.A." last Saturday, and trust some improvement may be brought about in the direction of our most needed article of diet. There is no reason why the supply should be limited when the farmers are having the time of their life in getting all their stock bought up at good remunerative prices. The time for artificial food stuffs has now passed, seeing the cattle have been put on the grass, of which there is a superabundance at this time. - P.B.P., NO. 2"

Issue: Saturday, 3rd June, 1916.

Presentation to a Stationmaster:

A pleasant function took place at Mr Boyd's Tavern on 26th ult., when Mr Allan Hamilton, late stationmaster at North Station, was made the recipient of a testimonial from the working men of Strathaven, on the occasion of his departure to take up a more important post at Scotstoun Station. Mr Wynn, C.C., in making the presentation, expressed the working men's great appreciation of the civility and respect shown to them by Mr Hamilton while stationmaster, and the high esteem in which he was held by one and all of the local workmen. He then handed to Mr Hamilton a handsome umbrella (with inscription), pipe, tobacco pouch (filled with tobacco), along with an umbrella for his wife. Mr Hamilton, in acknowledging the gifts, said that they would remind him of the people of Strathaven. He was pleased to know that whilst doing his duty he had been successful in not making any difference between gentle or semple, and begged to thank them one and all for their kindness. The following contributed to a most enjoyable evening's programme:- Messrs J. McLeavy, G. Cassidy, C. Mulligan, B. Horan, T. Robertson, G. Moffat, W. Frame, T. Moffat, D. Pentland, and Mr Anderson.

Issue: Saturday, 10th June, 1916.

Killed in Action:

Mr and Mrs John Knowles, 46 Ballgreen, Strathaven, have been notified that their son, Pte. Thomas Knowles, Argyll and Sutherland Highlanders, who was reported wounded and missing, is now reported to have been killed last September at the battle of Loos. He was 21 years of age, and enlisted at the outbreak of war. Prior to enlistment Pvte. Knowles was engaged in farm work.

Issue: Saturday 17th June, 1916.

Opening of Tennis Club:

It is pleasing to note that after all the Tennis Club is to remain in existence. A start was made for the season on Saturday, when the courts were formally opened by Mr Wm. Allan, B.Sc., in the presence of a large turn-out of players and friends. Mrs Broom served the first ball, after which games were carried on till dusk. Mr Allan treated the company to tea, his sister, Mrs Broom acting as hostess. The enthusiastic nature of the opening augurs well for the future of the club.

A Strathaven lad's first experience of India:

The following letter dated Kailana Camp, Chabrata, India, 27th April, 1916, from a member of the Garrison Battalion of the Scottish Rifles, a Strathaven lad, will doubtless be read with interest by many in the town:- *"On arriving at Bombay we had three days in train to Kampton Central Provinces, where we remained for six weeks. It is one of the hottest stations in India. Everything was all right, only the heat was something awful - fine bungalows, good rations, splendid orange and banana orchards, and the bazaar just at hand. Three weeks ago 250 of us were picked out for the hills. I, for one, was pleased - anything before yon heat (115 to 120 in the shade). Entrained on 15th, Great Indian Peninsular Railway, going about due north past Gwallor, Lucknow, to Delhi (old capital). Very flat barren country up to this, where we begin to climb, then the scenery opens for rock cuttings, forests and mountains. The Highland Railways at home are not in it. Parrots, monkeys, and beautiful birds in plenty are to be seen. Harvest in this part at present (corn, wheat, barley) all drop ripe, cutting with very small hooks, and threshing spreading with four bullocks, just the same as they did 1,000 years ago. Arrived at the terminus, Derhia Doon, on Wednesday night and went to our first rest camp. Off next morning, full marching order - did 12 miles first march; 22 miles second day; 24 third day; rested all day Sunday. Bathing in the R. Hoogley, swarming with silver trout. Started all again at 10 on baggage guard, 26 miles round the main road, climbing up the Oraig Brae all the time. Arrived at camp Monday, 2 o'clock, dead beat, getting a rest now for a few days. We are attached to the Rifle Brigade (English regiment), some Irish Rifles arriving shortly. This is one of the greatest sights ever I saw - hills all round. We are on the summit of one of the highest. Across from here is Chagala, another camp. Villages in every corner round and underneath. Every available patch is cultivated. The climate is just like very hot summer at home, cold at night. Just grand and uncommon after the place we have passed through. Hoping you are all in good health."*

"Stra'ven" Sunday Trading:

"Sir, - I have spent many a pleasant holiday in "Stra'ven," but this one is saddened and depressing owing to the gloom cast over the town through so many people one so often meets who have relations who have been killed or wounded at the war. The life's blood of the flower of the nation is being poured out to save us from being under the tyranny of a Prussian despot who would deprive us of all our dearly bought liberalisms. In the centre of the town there is a grave moral danger to the young people, and a large number of the residents are seriously alarmed about it. But the town, as such, is indifferent to the Sunday trading in refreshments. There is quite a fair trade all day long, which beats anything I have ever seen anywhere. I have counted from 150 to 300 young people enter one shop in an hour, and quite a crowd of young people are in the street near the shop eating and drinking much that is not for the good of their health. This trading goes on every day till near 12 o'clock at night, and for the benefit of the foreigner. How can such a thing be tolerated in the land of the Covenanters? Let the inhabitants rise up like men and follow the example of Rothesay and close up such places all day on Sunday and at a reasonable hour on week days. Rothesay Town Council altered their bye-laws to permit of opening four hours on Sundays, but owing to public opposition the Sheriff refused to ... the bye-laws and the shops remained closed. Let "Stra'ven" people do the same and have all these places closed all day on Sundays, and remove a black spot from their very doors. It is a credit to the people of "Stra'ven" that not one of them are found trading on Sunday ("Scotland's Day of Rest,) but they have opened their gates wide to admit the foreigner to do as he likes. See to it now that he does in future as you like, and as you also do. If foreigners do not respect the feelings of the people they come to live among they should have the decency to stay away.
ANNUAL VISITOR."

Issue: Saturday, 1st July, 1916.

Died on Service:

Mr James Barrie, saddler, Ballgreen, has received intimation that his son, Claude Barrie (Driver, R.F.A), died of fever in the East on 18th May. Claude was a native of Strathaven, and joined the colours about nine years ago, serving most of his time in India. When war broke out he was sent to France, then later to Mesopotamia. He was 30 years of age and a mason to trade.

Issue: Saturday, 8th July, 1916.

Strathaven and the War:

News reached Strathaven on Monday forenoon that another of our young townsmen, Corporal Alston Kyle, Special Brigade R.E., had died abroad from the effects of gas poisoning on 28th ult. He was 19 years of age, and was educated at Strathaven Academy, where he gained the dux medal. From there he proceeded to Hamilton Academy, then to Glasgow Technical College, where he studied chemistry, gaining a first class certificate. Prior to enlisting as a chemist in the R.E., he had completed his first year as a chartered accountant in the office of Messrs. Rattray Bros., Alexander & France, St. Vincent Street, Glasgow. In about a month after he left home he was in the trenches, and came through the Battle of Loos without a scratch. When his death occurred, he had been about eleven months abroad, and a sad feature of it is that he was being daily expected home on leave when the sorrowful news was received. He was of a quiet unassuming disposition, and much beloved by all who knew him. He took an active part in the work of the local Y.M.C.A. Great sympathy is felt for his sorrowing father, mother, and sister in their sad and sudden bereavement.

Issue: Saturday, 22nd July, 1916.

Failing to Report for Service:

At Hamilton J.P. Court on Saturday last, Patrick Porter, farm servant, West Newton, was charged with failing to report himself of service with the colours. The accused pled guilty, and was fined £2, with the option of 20 days imprisonment. He was handed over to the military authorities.

Issue; Saturday, 29th July, 1916.

Merchants' Association:

A meeting of the committee was held on Tuesday last, when in view of letter received in name of the ministers of the town, it was unanimously decided to recommend to the members that shops be closed on Friday to permit of merchants and their assistants attending the public service of intercession.

Second Anniversary of the outbreak of the War:

United services of intercession have been arranged to take place in the Parish Church on Friday.

At the one o'clock service the general public are invited to attend in their ordinary attire, and the large employers of labour have cordially agreed to extend the dinner hour. The Merchants' Association have also resolved that business premises be closed during the service, so that their employees may be able to be present. As on a former occasion it is expected that members of the Parish Council and School Board will be represented. The services will be conducted by the ministers of the town. - See advt.

Scholastic Appointment:

Miss Marion C. Mather, The Priory, has been appointed teacher in Low-Waters School under the Hamilton School Board, at a salary of £70.

Issue: Saturday, 2nd September, 1916.

Didn't Register:

At Hamilton J.P. Court on Tuesday, Robert Andrews, farm labourer, Todcastle, pled guilty with failing to register himself under the National Registration Act, accused was fined 10s or seven days.

All in the Day's Work:

A certain pathetic interest is attached to the following letter, the youthful writer of which succumbed to an attack of German gas in July last:- *"My Dearest Mary, - I have to thank you for your kind and welcome letter, which I received this afternoon. On Thursday evening I had just got nicely tucked in and was going off to sleep, when I was aroused by hearing the voices of our Company Commander and Sergeant-Major in the yard. Then I was surprised to hear them ascending the ladder, and the Sergeant-Major to say - "Prepare to move off in an hour's time - get everything packed up by that time. Then all was hurry and confusion. I hastily arose and dressed shoving all I could into a pack, and what I couldn't get into the pack, into sandbags. Meanwhile outside everything was astir - motor despatch riders arriving, and the engines of the transport wagons in full swing, men hurrying here and there busily loading the wagons with stores. No sooner had I learned that we were going to move off than I went post-haste round to a room I had hired from a French lady, where I had some of my most valued possessions. When I arrived there I made as big a commotion as I could at the front door, and was relieved on seeing the French lady's daughter at the window, who, on seeing who I was, immediately proceeded to dress and come down. I waited patiently. I explained to her in my most graphic French the circumstances in which I found myself, and apologised for awakening her at such a late hour (10.230 p.m. to boot). I proceeded in great haste to pack every conceivable article of mine into two sandbags which I had brought, while the French girl looked on, feeling rather sorry, no doubt, at losing me. Everything I shoved pell-mell in indescribable confusion into my sandbags, my main idea being to strip the room of everything we possessed. Then I hurried back to the farm "at the double," lugging at the sandbags with all my strength. The night was pitch dark, and though I knew my way, that did not prevent me from wallowing through every puddle-hole en-route. I arrived at the farm to find some of the Company already on parade. Blankets were being tied up in bundles of ten, according to instructions received, and neatly labelled with name, no of section, etc. Instead of their being carried laboriously down the ladder from the loft, I noticed they were being thrown, and almost invariably dropping with a splash into a pool of water conveniently situated at the foot of the ladder. People were busy ascending and descending the ladder, while officers and N.C.O.'s were exhorting the men to make haste and get on parade. With my coat, full equipment, and pack on, and carrying on my left arm, mackintosh, oil sheet, spare tunic; in my right hand holding two sandbags weighing nearly half cwt. a-piece, I "fell in" on parade. Waiting on the men arriving was a kind of torture for me, weights hanging on both my arms, and a heavy pack gripping on my back. I could hear sweeping going on up in the billet (evidently they were tidying up), and commands coming from the Q.M. Store, which was by this time nearly empty of what it formerly contained, and the motor lorries humming as if eager to be off. In the end, we did move, and I, feeling drowsy and weary, vaguely wondered where we were going, and how many "kilometres" I would have to march with these awful weights dragging on my arms . Then "halt," "about turn," "quick march," and we landed back to the billet again. We were formed up , and when our Commander said "This is only for practice, men," I could have dropped with chagrin. To think that I had gone to all this trouble for nothing! All this preparation for practice only. I at once made my way up to the loft and laid my equipment there. Meantime, blankets were being unloaded and distributed - the outside ones soaked and damp with the water. I got an inner pair (not mine), and as quickly as possible got off to sleep - 1 a.m. It was in the afternoon of the next day that I went round to see the French lady. She was delighted to see me, and kissed me, "a la francaise" first on the one cheek, then on the other. Poor lady! She had been crying that morning she thought we had gone! But that was not all yet. She told me how a lady had come in asking if we had gone and saying that she had two soldiers ready to take over our room. That was the last straw! Luckily, we were just in the nick of time. I could tell you how distressed she was at not having said "adieu" that night, and how pleased she was when we unexpectedly turned up, but now I must close. - I am, yours ever affectionately.* **Alston, B.E.F., France.**

Issue: Saturday, 9th September, 1916.

Killed in Action:

Mr John McCallum, Main Street, Strathaven, has been notified that his son Corporal Alex. McCallum, Cameronians (Scottish Rifles) has been killed in action. Cpl. McCallum was 20 years of age, and prior to enlisting was employed as a blacksmith.

Issue; Saturday, 16th September, 1916.

Bowling Club:

The directors of the club have been able to send £5 in aid of the Scottish Bowling Association Red Cross Funds. This sum was contributed by the players during the four last weekly promiscuous games arranged by the club on the Monday evenings.

Cricket:

Since the conversion of the Duke of Hamilton's residence at Dungavel into a Naval Hospital, nothing has been more interesting to the patients and townsfolk than the series of cricket matches which have been played - Dungavel versus Strathaven. The third of the series took place at Dungavel on Saturday. The pitch was fast and in fine condition. Strathaven went in first to bat, and were all out for 78, while the sailors were disposed of for 53 runs. The bowling and fielding of both sides far outshone the batting. Following the match, both sides sat down to tea, which was provided by the staff, and served in excellent style.

A Scholastic Success:

Mr James Young, son of the late Mr J. B. Young, S.S.C., of Beaconsfield, has been successful in winning a Royal Scholarship at the Imperial College of Science, South Kensington, London. This scholarship, of the value of £100 for three years, is one of the most valuable in the science side of education, and it has been held by many distinguished scientists. Mr Young entered from Allan Glen's School. And his success is the only one from the West of Scotland. For two years Mr Young has been assistant in the physics laboratory of the school and won the confidence of the headmaster. His success is not only a personal attainment, but an honour to the school and to Strathaven. We wish him every success in his career.

Issue: Saturday, 23rd September, 1916.

"Jack Cornwell" Memorial:

The pupils of the Academy on Wednesday had a collection in behalf of this worthy object, which is to endow a ward for disabled sailors and mariners in Queen Mary's Star and Garter House, Richmond, to be named after Jack Cornwell the boy hero of the battle of Jutland.

Issue; Saturday, 7th October, 1916.

Gallantry in the Field:

Strathaven's first Military Medal has arrived this week, the winner being Sergeant John Craig, Gordon Highlanders, who has been on service for two years. Sergt. Craig is 23 years of age, and is a son of Mr Robert Craig, Millar, Stonehouse Road. He joined the Gordon Highlanders at the outbreak of war, and has had many thrilling experiences at the front. Before the war he was employed at Hurst Nelson's, Motherwell.

Issue: Saturday, 14th October, 1916.

Mr John Ballantyne:

Mr John Ballantyne, late of Annandale, Strathaven, has been appointed assistant to chief goods manager on the Caledonian Railway. He resumed his new duties on October 3.

Issue: Saturday, 11th November, 1916.

Removing Pigs Without a License:

David McCarfrae, farmer, residing at Wee Cauldwalkening Farm, Strathaven, was charged at Hamilton J.P. Court on Monday with having removed from one schedule area to another eight young pigs without having a license authorising him to do so. In pleading guilty, Mr McCarfrae, though an aged man of 84, made such a vigorous plea in extenuation that the Fiscal felt compelled to admit that Mr McCarfrae's eye was not dimmed nor his natural strength abated. The Justices imposed the nominal penalty of £1, and allowed him a fortnight to pay.

Issue: Saturday, 18th November, 1916.

Mr George Sanders:

Mr George Sanders, lately booking clerk at Strathaven Central Station, died at his residence in Station Road on Tuesday evening, after a long illness. Deceased was highly respected by all who knew him. He leaves a widow and young son for whom the sympathy of the neighbourhood is felt.

Issue: Saturday, 25th November, 1916.

Soldiers' Parcels:

The sending of a congregational parcel now seems to be a recognised part of a church's work among the soldier lads, and the East Church seeks to raise funds for that purpose by holding a café chantant, sale and concert in the church hall. The concert is being arranged by Mr A. C. Hilston, and will be given by friends from without the town.

Honour to Belgian Soldier:

The friends of M Louis Debent, corporal in the Belgian Army, will be pleased to know of the military distinctions which have recently been conferred on him. He has been decorated Chevalier de l'Ordre de Leopold 11., and has also received the Croix de Guerre. Last month M Debent was wounded for the fourth time, and he is still in hospital abroad, where the presentation of his decorations took place last week. In honour of the occasion the Colonel in command gave a fete to the inmates of the ward, and M Debent received the felicitations of his comrades.

Issue: Saturday, 9ᵗʰ December, 1916.

Military Funeral:

As far back as the older residenters of the town can remember, there never was an opportunity presented to the inhabitants of witnessing the impressive spectacle of a military funeral. The personality of the young soldier had not a little to do with the large crowd of enthusiastic spectators who lined the streets en-route to the old Cemetery. Lance-Corpl. Wm. B. Howitt enlisted in the Seaforth Highlanders shortly after the outbreak of war and went to the front about 18 months ago and took part in many fierce engagements. He was fortunate to emerge from many of these life and death struggles until at the battle of the Somme, he was badly wounded in the region of the stomach with shrapnel. He lay in a hole for three days ere he was picked up, when he was hurriedly despatched to England and admitted to Dudley Road Military Hospital. Birmingham, where, after lingering for upwards of six weeks, the poor lad succumbed. His body was brought home on Thursday morning to the residence of his parents at 3 Chapel Road, and he was interred in the afternoon. To pay the last respect to a fallen comrade, a firing party from the H.L.I. at Hamilton Barracks was present under Sergt. Dickson. As the procession wended its way through the streets headed by the piper playing "The Flowers of the Forest," tears were brought to many eyes, while all business premises en-route were closed for the time being. Several soldiers on pass, including Captain Jennings and two Belgian soldiers, were present at the funeral, while the local Boy Scouts, under the Rev. M. U. Baird, were also in attendance. Rev. T. M. Dey conducted the service at the house and the graveside, where three volleys were fired, and "The Last Post" having been sounded, the grave was closed on another of the Great War's local victims.

Issue: Saturday, 30ᵗʰ December, 1916.

Presentation:

Mr John Hastie, manager of the Strathaven Co-operative Society, was made the recipient of a dressing case, and umbrella for Miss Hastie, from the employees on the occasion of his leaving Strathaven. Mr John Millar handed over the gifts on behalf of the employees. Mr Hastie, in acknowledging the gifts said he was sorry to depart from them. What is Strathaven's loss, however, is Busby's gain. A very enjoyable evening was concluded with the singing of "He's a jolly good fellow."

Conscientious Objector Fined:

A young warehouseman, 23 years of age, belonging to Strathaven, was on Tuesday in Hamilton J.P, Court charged with having failed to present himself at the Recruiting Office at Hamilton, and thus without leave of lawful excuse became an absentee, contrary to the Military Service Act. He admitted having received his papers, but had not reported himself. He said he was a conscientious objector, and that he had adopted this course as a protest against the action of the Tribunal in failing to administer the law. The Clerk of Court said they could not deal with that there. The Fiscal explained that the accused had been granted exemption for non-combatant service, but failing to do this he had rendered himself liable to be apprehended. He was arrested on Sunday, when he frankly stated he had not reported himself and what was his reason for not doing so. The Justices imposed a fine of £2, which they ordered to be retained from the army pay of the accused, who was handed over to the military authorities.

Hamilton Advertiser 1917

Issue: Saturday, 6th January, 1917.

Strathaven Working Party:

Mrs. Lee Dykes has despatched the following: Dec. 26: Cptn. Archibald Naismith, RAMC; Dec. 26: General Hospital Salonika - 8 shirts, 4 bedjackets, 6 mufflers, 4 caps, 12 vests, 40 prs socks, 2 suits pyjamas. Dec. 29: Matron No.5 General Hospital, Rouen 4 shirts, 5 vests, 2 sts pyjamas, 6 bed jackets, 30 prs socks, 9 bed socks, 4 mufflers, 4 caps, 1 pr mits; Dec.29: Mr. J. Shields, YMCA 40 prs socks.

Military Honours:

In the New Year's Army Honours' List appears the name of Captain Daniel Dougal, MD., RAMC., son of Doctor James Dougal, formerly in practice here. He is awarded the Military Cross for distinguished service in the field with the forces on the Somme after being mentioned in dispatches.

Issue: Saturday, 24 February, 1917.

Killed in Action:

Mrs Adam, Castle Street, Strathaven has now received word of the death in action of her brother Signaller John McArthur, Royal Scots Fusiliers previously reported missing on May 4th, 1916. He was killed by a shell on that date along with five of his comrades. Previous to his death Signaller McArthur had been eighteen months with the colours. He was 18 years of age and was the youngest son of Mr. A. McArthur, Kilmacolm, Renfrewshire.

Strathaven and the War:

It is with the greatest possible regret we announce the death from wounds received in action of Captain James Giffen, Cameron Highlanders. So far in the present war, Captain Giffen is Strathaven's most distinguished soldier, he having been raised from Company-Sergeant Major to Lieutenent in the field and been awarded the Military Cross at Festubert. His record since has been such as to bring him to the further notice of his superiors and he was promoted to the rank of Captain. The deceased was born and brought up in Thomson Street and served at the tailoring trade with Mr. Mason, Main Street. At 20 years of age he joined the Cameron Highlanders and in this regiment he had done all his soldiering. He came rapidly and prominently to the front as a gymnast and at an early age was gymnastic-instructor in his battalion. He went through the South African War and also travelled with his battalion in Egypt, India etc. His age was 32. Captain Giffen's death is much regretted in the locality and every sympathy is extended to Mrs. Giffen whose home is in Inverness.

Issue: Saturday, 10th March, 1917.

Killed in Action:

Mr John Mason, tailor, Bridge Street, Strathaven has received official intimation that his eldest son Private John Mason of the Scottish Rifles was killed in action on January 20th. Pvte. Mason who was well known locally was of a quiet and kindly disposition. He was 21 years of age and previous to enlistment was employed as assistant to Mr. Robert Thomson, grocer for nearly 6 years.

Issue: Saturday, 7th April, 1917.

Strathaven War Work Party:

Mrs Lee Dykes has, during the last two months, been sending out boxes each containing 12 pairs of socks, also cigarettes, to many of the local soldiers at the front to be distributed, and the letters of appreciation she has received show how very necessary warm hand-knitted socks mean to them in the trenches and marching. The following are a few extracts from some of the letters:- *"The contents were distributed to the men just a few hours before they went up the line for our last tour, and the fact that no cases of trench foot occurred during the period, I consider to be in no small measure due to the nice warm socks you and your generous helpers sent."* - C.T. *"I assure you we appreciate very much all that is being done for us, and are enabled to do our bit much better strengthened by the knowledge that we are not forgotten by those at home."* - B.P *"Such beautiful worm socks are exceedingly welcome just now, as we expect to go into the trenches again in a day or two, I thank you all most heartily."* - T.W. *"The box could not arrive at a more opportune time, as we are to do a week or ten days march, and it is then when good socks come to the rescue of the foot."* - A.T. *"I distributed the socks; the men all wish me to thank you and the Work Party for such an acceptable gift. It makes such a difference to have good, comfortable socks when marching . . . We are all loud in praise for the voluntary workers at home, we really appreciate your efforts. I sometimes think people at home imagine we do not do so sufficiently, but I am sure we do from the remarks made when marching on the benefit of good hand-knitted socks. I am sure you would all feel amply repaid for your efforts."* - J.H.M'R. The sailors also appreciated the socks, and said they had never had any so warm and comfortable. To three of the hospitals in Rouen and Dungavel, Mrs Lee Dykes has sent parcels containing 167 socks, 13 pyjamas, 16 shirts, 31 vests, 15 pants, 14 bed jackets, 25 mufflers, 22 caps, which she has had acknowledged.

Issue: Saturday, 21st April, 1917.

Military Medal:

Official information has just been received that Gunner Andrew Giffen of the Canadian Trench Mortar Group has been awarded the Military Medal for bravery in the field. He is the youngest brother of the late Captain James Giffen who won the Military Cross, and was promoted for distinguished service.

"Carrying On"

A few weeks ago there appeared under the Strathaven heading of the "Hamilton Advertiser" a paragraph on some young men having a smoking concert in Taylor's Hall. A copy of the paper was received by one of our local soldiers serving in France, and the following is an extract from one of his letters;- *"Hamilton Advertiser arrived alright. By the way, you should have heard the remarks in our hut over the paragraph in last week's Strathaven news about the young men having a convivial in Taylor's Hall. We should like to give these men (!) a few days out here."*

Awarded D.C.M:

Official news has been read by Mrs Wilson, 2 Castle Street, Strathaven that her son Gunner Henry Wilson has been awarded the Distinguished Conduct Medal for conspicuous gallantry and devotion to duty. He was serving with the colours in India when war broke out and immediately volunteered his services for France. Before enlisting he served his time as a blacksmith with Mr Prentice, Dunlop Street.

Issue: Saturday, 5th May, 1917.

Hamilton United Free Presbytery

National Service:

Arising out of the discussion at the previous meeting of the Presbytery on National Service and the prospect of ministers giving whole or part time to work under this scheme, the Rev. J.R. Forgan stated that since then he had read a communication from the War Emergency Service Committee, along with a special form to be filled up by ministers who might desire to take part in National Service, which form unlike the ordinary one, gave ministers an opportunity of offering part time. Ministers who wished to render service under the national scheme were advised to obtain this form and forward it, when filled up, to himself as convener of the Presbytery's War Emergency Committee, when it would be considered.

Musical:

At the recent school examinations of the Associated Board of the Royal Academy and the Royal College of Music, London Miss Peggie Bertram, "Annandale" passed successfully in the lower division. Miss Bertram is a pupil of Miss Mary J. Hamilton, LRAM "Shalimar."

Fatal Accident:

A sad cycling fatality occurred on Friday last. James Mather, son of Mr Mather, The Priory, and employee of Mr Dalgleish, grocer, fell off his bicycle in Townhead Street, his head striking the ground with great force. He was taken home in quite a conscious state, but succumbed to his injuries next morning.

The War in Africa:

Conductor William Walker Cochrane, S.A.S.C Transport attached S.A. Infantry has been awarded the medal of St. George (2nd class) with the following note in General Orders. "This W.O. who has always shown the greatest courage, on the 10th August, 1916, showed great bravery in getting forward the ammunition pack mules under heavy machine gun and rifle fire freely exposing himself regardless of danger. His fine personal example was of incalculable value in steadying the natives in charge of pack animals. He has always rendered great service in getting forward the ammunition packs." Conductor Cochrane who is the youngest son of the late James Cochrane, Walkers Bridge, has also been mentioned in dispatches.

Strathaven and the War:

Mr and Mrs Gavin Brown, Overton Road, have been informed that their son Private Robert Brown, Northumberland Fusiliers, was killed in action in France on 9th April. He was 22 years of age, and prior to enlisting was a plumber to trade - Bombardier Frank Craig, who enlisted at the outbreak of war in the Royal Field Artillery, and has been through most of the fighting in France has been reported killed. He was a son of Mr John Craig, Town Mill, and brother of Sergeant John Craig, Military Medallist - Mr Gilchrist, Gallowhill Farm, has also been notified that his brother Corporal William Gilchrist, was killed at Vimy Ridge. He came over with the Canadian Contingents, and was a son of the lat Mr Gilchrist, Silverigg.

Issue: Saturday, 12ᵗʰ May, 1917.

Killed in Action:

News has been received by Mr Cunningham, Thomson Street, that his son Private Robert Cunningham, Scottish Rifles, has been killed in action. He was 20 years of age and has other two brothers serving with the colours.

Issue: Saturday, 19ᵗʰ May, 1917.

Strathaven and The War:

Mr and Mrs Robert Craig, Millholm, Strathaven, have received official intimation that their son Corporal Frank Craig B.F.A was killed in action on 9 April, 1917. He was 22 years of age and was previously in the employment of William Fleming, Butcher, Strathaven. His brother, Sgt. John Craig, was recently decorated with the Military Medal - The name of Second Lieut. Claude Hamilton Napier, of Letham appears in the casualty list of wounded published on Thursday entered the army ay. He early in 1915.

Issue: Saturday, 26ᵗʰ May, 1917.

Toll of The War:

Mr and Mrs Davidson, Dunavon Lodge, have received official notification that their only son Private Donald Davidson, Seaforth Highlanders, has died of wounds in France. Prior to enlistment he was employed as assistant gardener to is father at Dunavon - Private Alex Taylor, H.L.I., son of Alex Taylor, baker, has also been reported killed, his parents receiving a letter from a soldier companion stating that Alex was killed by an explosion while in a shell-hole.

Issue: Saturday, 9ᵗʰ June, 1917.

Considerable Excitement was caused on the evening of Friday of last week owing to the advent of a runaway horse belonging to Mr Millar, butcher. The horse bolted from the slaughter-house and ran against the railings of Westdene, breaking a shaft of the van and damaging the wall. On receiving this check it changed its course, and came down Townhead Street, but owing to the broken shaft it was unable to take the attempted turn into Commongreen, and dashed in the shop window of Mr Watt, Jeweller, completely smashing one window and breaking the side of the other. The horse was badly hurt, and much damage done to the jewellery.

Issue: Saturday, 16ᵗʰ June, 1917.

Cycling Accident:

On Tuesday, while Mr J MacFarlane Paterson, writer, Strathaven, was cycling along the Lanark Road, between Crossford and Kirkfieldbank, the wheels of his cycle skidded and he fell heavily to the ground fracturing his skull and injuring his collar bone. Carried into a cottage nearby, the best of attention was given him, and he was promptly attended to by Dr. Hunter, Lanark, and Dr. Lindsay, Lochanbank. Dr. Mason was phoned for from Strathaven, and also the St. Andrew's Ambulance from Glasgow. Mr Paterson was removed home to his father's house at the Manse, Glassford, in charge of Dr. Mason.

Issue: Saturday, 23rd June, 1917.

General Intelligence:

In consequence of the war, Princes of the Royal Family who bear German titles are to relinquish these titles and adopt British surnames.

Strathaven Y.M.C.A. and Their Late Secretary:

At a meeting of the Strathaven branch of the Y.M.C.A. on 27/5/17, the president and various members made feeling reference to the death of their late secretary, Mr Alexander Taylor, a copy of which was sent to his parents. *"He was an enthusiastic member from the time he joined, and was very soon elected to the important post of secretary. In the discharge of his duties of secretary he proved himself a capable and sympathetic worker for the good of the branch. He had the interests of the meeting very much at heart, and when in any difficulty as to a speaker our secretary could always be relied on to find a way out. He was altogether an ideal member and secretary, and we have missed him and will continue to miss him. We would express to his parents and brothers and sisters our sympathy with them in their loss, which is also ours. On behalf of the Strathaven branch of the Y.M.C.A., D. F. Anderson, president, Alex Low, vice-president; Mungo Tennent, secy; James Young, treasurer, James McMillan."* It was reported in our issue of 26th ult., that Private Taylor was killed by a shell explosion while in a shell hole. This was erroneous. The War Office communication received last week reported him killed in action. Private Taylor, after serving his apprenticeship with his father, Mr Alex. Taylor, baker, Waterside and Bridge Streets, entered the service of the Union Bank, and had just completed his apprenticeship there when he joined the Army. As assistant secretary to Mr Mitchell of the Union Bank in connection with the local cattle show for the past three years he was well known to the farming community, who have generally expressed their sympathy.

Issue: Saturday, 30th June, 1917.

Strathaven and The War:

Mr William Kirkland, Barn Street, has received official word that his son, Sergt. Jack Kirkland of the Scottish Rifles, is missing since 14th April, 1917. He was called up on the 5th August, 1914, and after a few months training in Falkirk he went to France on the 19th March, 1916, and has been there ever since, having come through some very hard fighting. His brother George is in an hospital suffering from shrapnel wounds.

Two natives of Strathaven killed:

The late Private Morton (says the "Natal Witness" of 15th May,) who is officially accepted as dead on or since July 16 last, since which date he has been posted as missing was the eldest son of Mr and Mrs W. S. Morton. Alex, as he was familiarly known, was 19 years of age. He was educated at the Loop Street School and at Maritzburg College. He was at one time in the employ of Messrs Allison and Hime, in the City. When the call came to South Africa for recruits for the Overseas Contingent, he and his younger brother, James, known as Jimmy, were among the first to volunteer. Jimmy was wounded at Delville Wood, and made the supreme sacrifice at the Butte-de-Warlincourt on October 12 of last year. Both were extremely popular among a large circle of friends, and the deepest sympathy will go out to the bereaved family in this their double loss. The two lads were born in Strathaven, and visited their relatives on a short furlough in October, 1915.

Issue: Saturday, 14th July, 1917.

Strathaven - Scottish Concert:

Dr. Machardy has presented an interesting programme of Scottish songs, piano pieces and violin and piano music for Tuesday evening in Public Hall, Strathaven. He will be assisted by a variety of artistes. The entertainment should draw all patriotic music lovers to fill the house and enjoy an evening of splendid Scottish music.

Issue: Saturday, 21st July, 1917.

Glasgow Fair Holidays:

Never before in the history of Strathaven has such an influx of visitors been known. Not long since the inhabitants were very conservative in the letting of their homes during the summer months, but now the demand has been so great that all and sundry give up their houses for this purpose. There are at present over 2,000 incomers to the town, and many have been disappointed for the lack of further accommodation. The visitors are taking full advantage of the George Allan Public Park as a rest place, whilst the youngsters enjoy themselves on the swings, play at balls or "paddle" in the burn. This year the Hastie Park has been partly devoted to plots, the other part being given over for grazing purposes during the war. So far no special effort has been made for amusements in the Band Stand, except that given by the Stonehouse Silver Band last week on behalf of the Red Cross Fund. During the summer months the Strathaven Evangelistic Union hold an open air meeting at the Band Stand every Sunday afternoon(w.p). Last Sunday was a sight to be seen - the sloping banks from the band stand being literally covered with gaily dressed people. Short addresses and hearty singing is the feature of these meetings, in which several of the visitors take part. The many walks in the district are also much enjoyed.

Concert:

Dr. Robert Machardy must have been gratified by the reception his Scottish concert programme received from a musical audience mostly composed of Glasgow visitors, on Tuesday last. Misses Young, Jackson, and Smith sang a variety of gems of Scottish song, which, with Dr. Machardy's artistic accompaniments, were a delightful feature of the entertainment, and also a fine song, "Wallace the Brave," by Dr. Bell, encores being frequent. Miss P. Smith accompanied her sister, and played a piano piece artistically. Miss Bryson, A.B.C.M; who has passed with honours the British College of Music exam, was presented with a diploma, A.B.C.M. She played a Scottish military march, and a Scottish rondo, which was encored. Miss Hamilton, 11 years of age, played with skill, "Cuckoo Waltz," sang "The Laird o' Cockpen," for which she was encored, and also accompanied Dr. Machardy in "Freedom's Flag." Miss Murray, 11 years old, sang sweetly "I think of thee." Miss H. Wright, a juvenile, played prettily the "Kype Waltz" and two accompaniments. Dr. Machardy in his comments on musical talent said that such juvenile exhibitions of artistic talent were unknown upon the Continent and that we do not require Germans to teach us music. Miss Wright played with nimble touch the "Spinning Wheel," and sang "I lo'e na a laddie." Dr. Machardy, whose piano playing, singing, and numerous remarks on our duty to our country and to ourselves in musical matters received great applause, is to be congratulated upon the success of his music.

Law:

Mr Robert Wilson Park, apprentice with Messrs. Gebbie and Wilson, writers, has been successful in passing his second examination in general knowledge of the recent law agents' examination held in Glasgow.

The Holidays:

No more beautiful sight could be seen than that at the "Shoogly Brig" or Primrose Braes these fine summer days where the happy holidaymakers were their own purveyors - boiling their kettles, making their own tea, as many of them tipped the bare or paddled in the burn. The roving commission given to all and sundry to these delightful places has helped to make Strathaven the great summer resort that it has become. The weather has been everything that could be desired and full advantage has been taken of outdoor amusements, such as bowling, tennis, fishing, and a few found pleasure on the golf course. The meeting held in The George Allan Park on Sunday afternoon last was a sight not easily to be forgot; and we believe many will carry home with them sweet memories of happy days spent at Strathaven.

Issue: Saturday, 11th August, 1917.

Strathaven and The War:

News has been officially received by Mr Andrew Semple, Commercial Road, stating that his son Private William Semple, Scottish Rifles, was killed in action near Palestine. He was 24 years of age, and employed as a tailor with Mr J.D. Findlay previous to joining the army - official word has been received that Private Hugh Irvine, H.L.I., eldest son of Mr Alex Irvine, 23 Kirk Street, was killed in action in France on 10th July. He was 26 years of age and previous to enlisting was employed with Lamond Bros., Threshing Mills. His wife and family reside at 7 Green Street.

Issue: Saturday, 18th August, 1917.

Fatal Accident:

On Thursday last, 9th August, a lad named Thomas Robertson, aged 13 years, son of Mr Thomas Robertson, pony driver, 50 North Street, met with a sad accident by falling from a wall about eight feet high at the rear of the dwelling house in North Street. He was removed to the Western Infirmary suffering from concussion on the brain, and died on Saturday morning.

Loyal Colonels:

Alexander Whyte, who was a police constable for some time in Strathaven, and emigrated to Australia about seven years ago is now in France with the Australian Army. He and his second son (Alex) enlisted together in Perth (Western Australia) and were together in France. We regret to learn that the son was killed while in action on 15th July, 1917. He was 20 years of age, and was engaged at farm work previous to enlisting.

Storm:

During the past week we have been experiencing torrential showers of rain, while thunder has been rumbling about for several days, which culminated on Wednesday evening with a terrible crash, without warning, as though one or other of the church spires, had tumbled over, giving a faint idea of what an air raid would be. So far as known no damage has been done to the crops, which are looking their best and with a little sunshine the corn will be ready for cutting.

Captain Alan E.G. Leadbetter RHA:

We regret to announce, was killed in action on 4th August. He was the third son of Mr Greenshields-Leadbetter of Stobieside by his marriage with Mary, daughter of the late Sir John Usher of Norton and Wells, Baronet, and was born on 28th August, 1896. Captain Leadbetter was educated at Ardvreck and Rugby, and at the Royal Military Academy, and received his commission in February 1915. In May of the same year he took out a draft to Gallipoli, and soon after became Orderly Officer to his Colonel. He served as Adjutant to his brigade till the evacuation of Helles, and was mentioned in dispatches *"for gallant and distinguished services."* He served on the Western front till November 1916, when he was wounded, and was at home for some months. He returned to his old battery as a Captain, and commanded it for two months, when he was attached to - Battery, R.H.A., and after commanding it for a month he was killed on 4th August by an enemy shell, His Colonel writes - *"I cannot express to you how universally his loss will be mourned by all ranks, for I seldom met anyone more beloved and at the same time admired and respected. He was attached to . . . battery, and I was hoping very much to get him permanent command of it, as in spite of his youth he made an ideal battery commander. Alas! It seems to be always our best and most promising who are taken."* Another Colonel under whom he served writes - *"The chance of commanding a Home Artillery battery in a big battle very seldom falls to the lot of so young an officer. I have never met any one of his years with such brilliant promise. He was a born leader."* Mr Greenshields-Leadbetter's only surviving son is serving in Palestine, attached Imperial Camel Corps. Captain Greenshields-Leadbetter was greatly beloved by all his friends, and his sad loss is greatly deplored in Avondale, where at Stobieside he spent many happy days of his boyhood among the hills. The deepest sympathy is felt for his parents and family in their sore bereavement.

Issue: Saturday, 25th August, 1917.

Sailors Entertained:

On Wednesday afternoon, about 30 sailors from Dungavel Naval Hospital were entertained at the local Picture House. The pictures were of a first-class variety and thoroughly enjoyed by the tars. A nice tea was served at an interval in the programme. Each sailor received a packet of cigarettes on entering.

Strathaven and The War:

Mr A. Watson, 6 Almada Street, Hamilton, has been notified that his brother Pte. Robert Watson, Cameron Highlanders, who was reported missing since 12th October, 1916 is now believed to have been killed on that date. He was the youngest son of the late John Watson, Commercial Road, and before enlisting was employed in the grocery department of the Co-operative Society. He was 19 years of age.

Issue: Saturday, 1st September, 1917.

Bowling Club and Wounded Soldiers:

"Sir, The committee of the Strathaven Bowling Club, I am informed, held a meeting on Monday night to consider whether they should give an entertainment to the wounded sailors from Dungavel, but the would be patriots, who have enjoyed themselves all summer, were evidently afraid the men, who had risked their lives and suffered for their country, might spoil their green, so the proposal, I understand, was turned down. Surely Strathaven has soon grown weary in well-doing:- Hopeful."

Open-air Concert:

On Wednesday night some girls and boys belonging to Flemington got up a very successful open-air concert in aid of the Princess Louise Hospital for Limbless Soldiers and Sailors, which was given in the back green at Overwood Place. The programme, which was a large and varied one, was greatly enjoyed by a large audience. At the end of the programme three ladies and one gentleman contributed also. The amount gathered was £1.12s.2d. The effort was entirely the children's own, and reflects great credit on them.

War Fund Operetta:

From advertisement under the above heading it will be observed that the committee which so successfully managed the operetta last year in aid of war funds intend running another for the same laudable object. The piece to be taken up is entitled "The Magic Ruby," and on this occasion it will be confined solely to boys and girls between the ages of 10 and 17 years. This committee has already disbursed about £150 for the war relief fund during the last three years - a truly creditable sum. Recognising the great and indispensable co-operation which parents offered in the past by sending their children to take part in these performances, the committee make a further appeal to parents to assist in making the coming performances a record both for pleasure and profit. Practices will be commenced on Wednesday evening first.

Absent from Army - Peculiar Case:

In Hamilton J.P. Court on Saturday - before Bailie Gunn and Mr M Blair - George Donald, private in the Scottish Rifles, was charged with having on 13th July absented himself without leave from his regiment at Hamilton. He was apprehended at West Cauldcoats, Avondale, on 16th August, Donald pled not guilty and was found not guilty.

Strathaven Golf Club (Ltd):

A meeting of the shareholders presided over by Mr James Barrie, was held in the Lesser Public Hall on Monday evening, to consider the financial situation of the company. The Chairman explained that Mr Pollok, the landlord, had made an offer to the club to take the course off their hands with a view to the ground being put under the plough, and to relieve the club of any compensation for injury to the ground or fences. A committee of the club had formerly considered this, but they felt it was a matter which more concerned the shareholders. Since the beginning of the war the company had been run at a serious loss, which was likely to continue for the duration of the war. This is partly accounted for by the heavy war taxation, and partly owing to a loss of members because of the war. Were the company wound up at present, however, the shareholders would practically receive back all their capital, whereas, if Mr Pollok's offer were declined, they were faced with a continuous drain on the money on hand and the prospect that at the end of the lease - five years hence - they would have to meet a claim for compensation with their funds exhausted, unless at that time a new lease could be arranged. The meeting, which was well attended, was unanimously of opinion that the loss of the golf course would be a great misfortune and a blow at the prosperity of Strathaven. The improved train service was obtained largely because of its formation , and when a deputation met Mr Mathieson, the railway manager, he put great stress on the existence of the golf course, and exacted an informal promise that as soon as the company saw their way an 18-hole course should be formed and thus attract additional visitors. Before coming to any final decision in the matter, the meeting agreed to make an appeal to shopkeepers, and to those who are in the habit of letting their houses, to come to the assistance of the club during the war, and with a view to making that easy, it was decided to create an honorary membership at an annual fee of 10s for gentlemen and 5s for ladies. A personal call will be made within the next month with the view of getting their support, and it is hoped a generous response will be made to this appeal.

Issue: Saturday, 22nd September, 1917.

Accident:

While engaged in harvesting work on Wednesday, 12 September, in the employment of Mr Lindsay, West Dykehead Farm, Catherine Pirie, domestic servant, aged 16, slipped in front of the reaping machine. Her right leg was severely cut and she has received compound fracture of the ankle joint. She was attended by Dr. Mason and removed to the Western Infirmary, Glasgow.

Sixty years a 'Fremason':

A special meeting of Lodge "St. Andrew" No.215 was held on Saturday evening last, 15th inst., when two brethren were passed to the Fellowcraft Degree by Br. John Telfer. The occasion was memorable from the fact that Bro. John Sommerville, who has been Tyler of this Lodge for the last 50 years, completed his 60th year as a Freemason. It has been decided to recognise Br. Sommerville's long and active connection with the craft in a suitable manner, and contributions for this purpose will be gladly received by Bro. Robert Thomson, Townhead Street, Strathaven.

Issue: Saturday, 29th September, 1917.

War Work Party:

Mrs Lee Dykes begs to acknowledge with many thanks the sum of 7s received from Miss Peggy Barclay from the sale of scent sachets. The weekly meeting of the War Work Party will commence on Tuesday, 2nd October, from 2.30 to 4 o'clock. All those who are wishful to help in knitting socks and making other garments for our sailors and soldiers contact Mrs Lee Dykes.

War Honour:

Mr W. H. Wilson, of Todshill, Strathaven, has received word that his son, Private Duncan Wilson, Durham L.I., has been awarded the Military Medal. His commanding officer, congratulating him, says:- *"It is the opinion of the Colonel and myself that you have done more than could even be expected of any runner, and you have been decorated with the Military Medal, which you so thoroughly deserve."* Pte. Wilson joined the army on the 10th August, 1914, and was wounded on the 16th September, 1916, the second day of the tanks. He has now been wounded a second time, August 22nd, 1917 - gunshot wound in the face and part of his lower jaw blown away. His father, who has been receiving word daily from the matron has just been advised that he is now out of danger. His younger brother was wounded in July, and is now convalescent. He is in the Scottish Rifles.

War Work for Winter:

At a meeting of the teachers of the Church Girls' Industrial Class held in Dhu Crag Manse it was agreed to continue to make comforts for our soldiers . The class is now enrolled as a branch of the Women's Volunteer War Workers' Association, and this ensures that all comforts reach the men who are in greatest need. In view of the approach of winter, it was agreed to begin work earlier this year, and the opening meeting will be held in the Church Hall on Thursday first, 4th October, at 7.15 pm. It is hoped that many will take this opportunity of doing so good a service, and an invitation is given to all girls from ten years upwards. A special class is formed for older girls. Instead of prizes it was agreed to grant a certificate to all who make sufficient attendance, stating that they had worked for the soldiers. As the cost of material is greatly increased, an appeal is made for financial assistance. Mrs Baird is president and treasurer, but subscriptions will be received by any of the teachers, or by the Rev. M. U. Baird.

Issue: Saturday, 6th October, 1917.

Merchants' Association:

A special meeting of members was held in the Public Hall on Monday last - Mr Adam Grierson presiding over a good attendance. Mr W.C. Blake reported as to the favourable response given by the shopkeepers to the appeal in connection with the Golf Club. A report was also given in as to the result of the canvass regarding the closing of shops on Saturdays during winter at 8 p.m. In view of the large majority in favour of this course it was unanimously agreed to close shops on Saturdays at 8 p.m. as from today's date.

War Relief Fund - Strathaven Soldier's Gallantry Recognised:

On Thursday last, at a meeting of the Executive Committee in the Council Offices, Company Sergt. Major G. McCallum, Cameron's, was presented with a gold watch bearing the following inscription - *"Presented by Avondale War Relief Fund to 4314 Company Sergt. Major G. McCallum, Cameron Highlanders, who was awarded the Distinguished Conduct Medal for conspicuous gallantry and resource while in command of a trench. Also for extinguishing a petrol fire by rolling in it saving many lives, but being severely burned in the act. - 15th March, 1915,"* The Chairman, Mr Cameron, in a very happy speech said how pleased the Stra'ven folks were at having the opportunity of recognising the bravery and disregard of personal consequences shown by Company Sergt. Major McCallum, who had the best wishes of all, and who no doubt would in the near future deserve further honours. In the local list of honours awarded there were eight names, and of these three had already been acknowledged. The other would be recognised as opportunity offered. Sergt. Major McCallum is the son of the late Mr George Young, Newton Farm, and enlisting under the name of McCallum has seen service all over the world for twenty years - Africa, China, India, and in the present war in different countries. Sergt. Major McCallum feelingly replied, and by special request gave a short and most interesting account of the events which led to his receiving the D.C.M. Most of those present, including some personal friends, voiced their appreciation of Sergt. Major McCallum's services, recalling many happy reminiscences of his early boyhood in Strathaven, and a very pleasant evening was spent.

Issue: Saturday, 13th October, 1917.

The Girls' Industrial Class, which meets in the East Church Hall every Thursday evening for the purpose of making comforts for the sailors and soldiers, has now resumed for the session. A cordial invitation is given to all girls of 10 years and over to come and help in this fine work.

Parish Council of Avondale:

The monthly meeting was held on Tuesday. Present - Messrs Andrew Barr, W. R. Brown, R. R. Galloway, John Wiseman, William Wright, Patrick Wynn, and Wm. Dykes, chairman. As recommended by the Works Committee, some necessary repairs are to be executed at the Cemetery House, and the wages of employees are unanimously increased 2s weekly as war bonus, on the motion of Mr Barr, seconded by Mr Wynn. The allotments in the Hastie Park and Allison Green are to be re-let for 1918 at 2s.6d each, as presently. The weekly allowance to all in receipt of relief was unanimously increased 1s to single cases up to 4s for families and one pair boots was granted to each child on the roll. Receipt of £265 Government grant under the Agricultural Rating Act was intimated and Poor Law business was considered, accounts amounting to fully £189 being passed for payment.

Avondale School Board:

The usual monthly meeting was held in the Board Room on Tuesday. Dr. Mason, chairman of the Board, presided. The Clerk submitted a circular from the Department as to the grain in aid of teachers' salaries and a note of the amount allocated to this Board, with a form to be filled up and submitted for the Department's approval. Stating what amount the Board were prepared to contribute by way of supplementing the Department's contribution. It was decided, as the matter was important, that a special meeting should be held on Tuesday, 23rd October, to consider the matter further, and that the clerk should meantime ascertain what other Boards propose to do. The clerk also submitted some communications received by him as to the formation of a Cadet Corps in connection with the Academy. It was decided to consider this matter also at the special meeting.

Issue: Saturday, 20th October, 1917.

War Work Party:

Mrs Lee Dykes begs to acknowledge with many thanks the following sums, raised by the sale of lavender bags: Miss Ella Frame, 9s; Miss Ginty Forbes, 18s.8d; Miss Janet Allan, 10s.10d.

Issue: Saturday, 27th October, 1917.

Successful Concert:

A successful concert was held in the West United Free Church Hall on Thursday night to provide parcels for the soldiers. The following artistes contributed in a highly creditable manner: Miss McRoberts, contralto; Miss Guthrie, violinist; Misses Fleming and Baxter, elocutionists; Miss Barbara Hamilton, pianist; Mr Stewart, baritone; and concertina and banjo selections by Messrs Wilson and Brown. The church choir rendered several part songs in a pleasing manner, and members of the choir also contributed with solos and duets. The collection taken amounted to £7, and was handed over to the Church Guild Society.

Considerable Excitement:

Considerable excitement was caused in Strathaven on Wednesday morning by the sight of three aeroplanes hovering over the town, and their final descent into the field adjoining Lethame House. The school children, who were just gathered into line, were so excited and anxious to see the aeroplanes that they were accorded a half-holiday, and immediately rushed off to the field. Most of the children had never viewed one before, except in the air, and when one of the aviators gave a display in looping the loop, etc., their excitement knew no bounds. Unfortunately the weather broke down, but in spite of that, practically the whole town turned out to see the aeroplanes. The cause of the descent was engine trouble with one of the machines, and owing to the weather the airmen, who were flying from Edinburgh to Ayr, were forced to postpone their departure till Thursday. After another little display they left amid ringing cheers from the school children, who had congregated to witness the commencement of their interrupted flight.

Mutual Improvement Association:

The usual weekly meeting was held on Monday night. Mr Wm. Ferguson presided over a small attendance. No doubt the stormy night kept many people indoors, but those who ventured out were well rewarded by the address Mr Anderson, Stonehouse, had prepared for them. Mr Anderson took for his subject, "International Relations." After a few remarks on the Hague Conference, which had proved such a failure in dealing with important disputes between nations, the lecturer gave several suggestions of how peace might be brought about and maintained. Not one of the suggestions, however, fitted in with present-day requirements. The German people must become democratic, Prussian militarism must be stamped out, and German autocracy done away with. The lecturer's closing remark that democracy does not wage war on democracy roused criticism, several members present being inclined to doubt this. After a few appreciative remarks by Mr Cameron, C.C., Mr Watt, Mr D.F. Anderson, and the Chairman, a very hearty vote of thanks was accorded the lecturer.

Issue: Saturday, 3rd November, 1917.

Farm Sale:

Considerable public interest was aroused by the sale of the farm of Brownside, which took place in the Public Hall on Tuesday last. The lands belonging to the late Mr James Cochran, and extend to about 200 acres; rental and valuation roll, £252. The upset price was £5,000. After considerable competition the subjects were knocked down at £5,760 to Mr Robert Warnock, farmer, Netherholm. Mr James Allan of the Strathaven Auction Market, Ltd., was auctioneer, and Messrs Gebbie & Wilson, writers, acted as agents in the sale.

Strathaven and the War:

Official news has been received that Gunner John Park of the Royal Garrison Artillery, son of the late John Park, builder, and of Mrs Park, Springknowe, Strathaven died at St. John's Ambulance Brigade Hospital, Etaples, in France, on 25th October, from the effects of shell-wound on the head received on the 19th October. Gunner Park was on sentry duty when he received the fatal wounds, and had just been three days back at his gun after being wounded for the first time. He was buried on the 26th October in Etaples Military Cemetery.

Rainfall:

From the records kept at East Overton, the total rainfall registered in August, September, and October of this year amounts to 16.48 inches there being only 18 days in all in which no rain fell. Such continuous rain at this time of the year is without precedent in this locality. In the corresponding period last year there were 41 dry days recorded: in 1915, 62; and 1914, 56; and the average for many years past is about 50 dry days in these three months. For the first seven months of this year the rainfall was exceptionally light, amounting to only 16.59 inches.

Farm Servant Forfeits Wages:

Recently James Cassie raised an action in the Small Debt Court against his master, Wm. Steel, farmer, Caldergreen, Strathaven, for £6.6s.8d being two months' wages due as at 28th July, 1917. The defence was a denial of the claim, and a counter claim for damages was lodged. The case went to proof on 26th October, and after evidence had been led Sheriff Shennan, in granting absolved, with expenses, in favour of the defender, while dismissing the counter claim, indicated the law on the subject, and stated in view of the circumstances of the case, and the fact that the servant left in the midst of the hay harvest, that the forfeiture of his wages was not too severe a penalty to be attached to his conduct. Agent for pursuer - Mr John Cassells, solicitor, Hamilton; agent for defender - Mr J. McFarlane Paterson, solicitor, Strathaven.

Mutual Improvement Association:

The weather on Monday evening was again responsible for a poor attendance. Mr Watt presided, and after the minutes of the previous meeting had been read and approved, he briefly introduced the lecturer for the evening, the Rev. Mr Muirhead, who had taken for his subject "Reminiscences." In his opening remarks the lecturer said that a more appropriate title might have been "Random Recollections." These recollections were divided into four distinct periods - childhood's days, holidays, college days, and finally his early years as a minister. The childhood period was briefly passed over, and then we journeyed with the lecturer to Ireland and had quite an interesting lesson in geography. After several amusing stories concerning the Irish, the lecturer gave a short outline of University life. Mr Muirhead's most interesting period, however, dealt with the time when he was parish minister at Weststruther, and his stories about Lady John Scott kept the audience highly amused.

Rev. M. U. Baird, M.A.

By appointment of the U.F. Presbytery of Hamilton, the Rev. M. U. Baird was granted leave of absence from his charge in Strathaven to take up work at Rosyth in the month of July. The following is an extract from the "Dunfermline Press" of Saturday last: *"The large audience which assembled in the Presbyterian Church on Thursday evening to bid farewell to the Rev. Matthew Urie Baird, whose term of office as minister of the church expires tomorrow, was eloquent testimony to the popularity which Mr Baird has attained in the Garden City. It was more than a purely congregational meeting, for numbered amongst those present were many members of other denominations who, by association with him in other than a church capacity, have learned to esteem the worth of the minister of the "Scotch Church," as the Presbyterian place of worship is familiarly referred to by the English residents of the town. After a service at tea at an interval in a fine musical programme, Mr Miller, on behalf of the congregation, asked Mr Baird's acceptance of a drawing-room clock. He paid Mr Baird the compliment of having adjudged him, on short acquaintance, to be a man who was determined to do everything he could to make the church at Rosyth a success. The congregation, Mr Miller, was sure, would follow Mr Baird's future career with interest and with good wishes, (applause.) Mrs King, also on behalf of the congregation, presented Mrs Baird with a beautiful gold watch, suitably inscribed. Mr Baird was received with quite an ovation when he rose to acknowledge the gifts and eulogiums bestowed upon Mrs Baird and himself. He said he was particularly gratified that they had recognised Mrs Baird, for to her had fallen the important task of keeping the home fire burning at Strathaven. They could scarcely realise the extent to which the success of his work at Rosyth had depended upon his wife. (Hear, Hear.) Both he and his wife accepted the gifts with pride and gratitude, and they left behind them many pleasant memories. Thereafter Mr Gill said that Mr Raper and he had been deputed by the Rosyth Ratepayers' Association to convey their thanks to Mr Baird for what he had done in spheres outside the church. Rosyth people, he added, would always remember with gratitude what Mr Baird had accomplished for the educational interests of the community. In addition to the above, the Bible Class presented Mr Baird with a silk M.A. hood.*

Issue: Saturday, 10th November, 1917.

Picture House:

After being closed down for several months the Cinema House was re-opened this week under new management. The programme included some of the finest films ever exhibited in Stra'ven. Pathe's Gazette of the war is always a great attraction, and the long drama "Arms and the Woman" is a beautiful and entrancing picture. As will be seen from our advertising columns that popular serial "Pearl of the Army" will commence next Friday. We understand the promoters propose showing a high-class programme each week.

Issue: Saturday, 17th November, 1917.

Ambulance Work:

For several years a successful ambulance class has been conducted at the station under the auspices of the St. Andrew's Ambulance Association. Formerly the class was confined to males, but something in the nature of an innovation has taken place this year by the introduction of a mixed class. The advisability of possessing a knowledge of ambulance work is always apparent, but in these days of war it seems more than ever desirable that such a knowledge should be acquired by all, and nowhere can this be more easily obtained than under the able tuition of Dr. Mason, who conveys his instructions in a kindly manner and simple language, thus rendering the studies easy and interesting.

Parish Council of Avondale:

The monthly meeting was held on Tuesday, all the members being present - Mr William Dykes in the chair. Receipt was intimated of £100 from the trustees of the late Miss Agnes Gebbie, and it was decided to invest it in the 5% War Loan for five years. On the motion of Mr Barr, seconded by Mr Brown, it was unanimously agreed to reopen the John Hastie Park, the grazing season being over. On the motion of Mr Galloway, some trees are to be replanted in the George Allan Park, and some repairs at the Holm Street bridge were remitted to the Works Committee. Poor Law business having been considered, accounts amounting to £497.17s.8d were passed for payment.

Issue: Saturday, 24th November, 1917.

Picture House:

This house is being well patronised, and the management are showing really first-class pictures. Good order is being maintained, and the pictures are clean, clear, and steady. The first episode of that popular serial, "Pearl of the Army," was shown last week, and will undoubtedly proved a great attraction. For next week's programme see advert.

Prisoners of War:

The War Office has sanctioned a "Personal Parcel" scheme, whereby our prisoners of war in the hands of the enemy may receive a parcel every quarter from relatives at home. Since the scheme of the Central Prisoners of War Committee came into operation last year, it has not been possible for relatives or friends to send parcels. All food parcels are now sent through the Care Committee of the duly authorised associations, while clothing, etc., is supplied by the Regimental Committees. The new scheme, which comes into operation on 1st December, authorises the sending of certain parcels every quarter by relatives of the interned men. That the privilege will be much appreciated, goes without saying, The difficulty is to get the relatives of the unfortunate men to understand thoroughly how to proceed in the matter and to note most carefully what may be sent. Any deviation in the matter of the contents of the parcel may lead to its confiscation.

In the first place, a coupon, without which no parcel can be sent, must be applied for. The next-of-kin of the prisoner has the right to the coupon or to designate the prisoner to whom it is to be given. The coupon is furnished on application to the secretary of the Care Committee of the regiment to which the man was attached when he was taken prisoner. If in doubt as to the source of application, an inquiry at the Post Office, where a list of Prisoners of War Associations are kept, will secure the proper information. The parcel to be sent must weigh not less than 3lbs and not more than 11lbs. It should be packed in a cardboard box and should have thereon the correct address of the prisoner written or printed on the outside. The address should give the number, rank, name, coy and battalion of regiment, together with his prison number (if any) and name of prison camp in Germany. The parcels must not contain eatables, with the exception of sweets. Any of the undernoted articles may be enclosed:- pipe, sponge, pencils, tooth powder (paste is not allowable), pomade, cap badge and badges of rank, shaving brush, safety razor, bootlaces (mohair and not leather), pipe lights, housewife, handkerchiefs (one a quarter), shaving soap (one stick a quarter), health salts, insecticide powder, braces and belts (provided they are made of webbing and include no rubber or leather), combs, hair brushes, tooth brushes, cloth brushes, buttons, chess, draughts, dominoes, dubbing, hobnails, sweets, medal ribbons, brass polish, mufflers (one a quarter), mittens (one pair each quarter). It should be carefully noted that any article not mentioned in the above list should not be included. Failure to comply with these instructions will lead to the confiscation of the parcel. When packed and ready for despatch the parcel should be taken to the Post Office. (The parcel must be securely packed, and the coupon received through the Care Committee must be affixed to it.) A fresh coupon must be applied for every quarter if relatives desire to take advantage of the new scheme.

War Work Party:

Mrs Lee Dykes wishes to gratefully acknowledge with many thanks the following sums - Avondale War Relief Fund, £100, sale of photos, per Mr J.S. Duncan, 5s; Misses Jeanie Fleming and Mary Allan, Hallowe'en, 6s; Miss Charlotte Pettigrew and Master John Cunningham, £1; Miss Mary Healy, Jessie Wiseman, and Janet Hamilton, 9s1d; Misses Sarah Glance and Agnes Wiseman, 11s.2d; Misses and Masters Downie and Frame, £2.13s4d; Two Young Ladies, 7s; Misses May Wilson and Jeanie Park, sale of gollywogs £1.2s.

Issue: Saturday, 1st December, 1917.

Schoolboys Charged:

Three schoolboys were charged on Saturday last with breaking open and retaining contents of two ambulance boxes in a guard's van at Strathaven Station. The parents paid the value of damages done on articles stolen, and the case was continued till the last Saturday in February.

Donaldson Soup Kitchen:

The soup kitchen resumes on Monday first, 3rd inst., in the vacant building at corner of Green Street and Barn Street. Children are asked to make application to the headmaster and headmistress. Gifts in kind and subscription will be gratefully received. The secretary and treasurer is Mr John Torrance.

An Appeal for Gifts:

An appeal for gifts of sweets to be given as xmas presents to the men in the Hut where she had been working has been made by Mrs Dey on her return from France. The following week the girls of Rankin U.F. Church brought 131 gifts of sweets, each packet done up in a little bag of brightly-coloured silk or in khaki handkerchief, and each containing a beautiful Xmas card.

Sphagnum Moss War Dressings:

Every Thursday evening the Rankin Church Hall presents the appearance of a busy bee-hive filled with eager girls in their dainty uniforms of snow-white caps and aprons, bending patiently over the laborious work of making moss dressings. Many of the workers wear war work badges for long service, and the extent of their labours is shown by the fact that since the month of March, 2,873 war dressings, mostly of large size, and 66 pillows have been despatched to the Deport for Lanarkshire at Rutherglen.

Mutual Improvement Association:

The lecturer on Monday night was Mr John Semple, Lanark. His paper was entitled "Coals and Culture," but this was really a misnomer, the lecturer himself pointed out. The paper dealt with that very wide subject - labour and the cultivation of the intellect - and the lecturer put forward several suggestions whereby the lot of the working man might be improved. More leisure, a standard minimum wage, continuity of employment, a more healthy environment, and last - but by no means least important - a better education for the young, were among the suggestions.

Drumclog Concert:

The annual event took place in Drumclog School on the evening of 23rd ult. Favoured with fine weather, the school was packed to its utmost. The chair was very ably occupied by Mr William Dykes, Hazliebank, supported by Mr Thomas A. Findlay, High Drumclog. The following artistes from Strathaven delighted a very attentive audience with their solos, duets and quartets - Messrs Brown, Hilston, Leggat and Wilson, Misses Brown, Fleming Leggat, and Tennant. Miss Tennant very ably officiated at the piano. Two songs by Master William Meikle, were much enjoyed, and some readings by Miss Susan Fleming were fully appreciated. An assembly followed the concert, which was well patronised, the music being supplied by Messrs Gray, Morton, and Taylor. As a result of their concert, the committee will be enabled to hand over the sum of £7 10s to the local War Relief Fund.

Women's Work in France:

The opening meeting of the Y.W.C.A., was held in the Rankin Church Hall on 29th ult., when Mrs Dey gave an address on "Women's Work in France." After referring to the magnificent work done by nurses, ambulance drivers, and motor drivers, she gave a particular description of a visit which she paid to a camp of Women's Auxiliary Army Corps. This camp occupied a beautiful situation overlooking a fine prospect of river, woodlands, and sea. Part of the grounds was laid off as a hockey field, another part as tennis courts, and there was a prospective garden. Mrs Dey was personally conducted over the camp by the Commanding Officer, who showed with great pride the excellent dormitories, the bathrooms, with good supplies of hot and cold water (a real luxury in France), the kitchen, the laundry, the mess-room with its wooden tables scrubbed snowy-white, the recreation room, and the "sick bay." where sick girls are carefully tended by a trained nurse. A Canteen Hut has been erected by the Y.M.C.A., and soon it will be opened and staffed by the Y.W.C.A. ladies. Everything is done to keep the girls as fit as possible, and though they have long hours and strenuous work, they enjoy the privilege of "doing their bit" to help to bright the war to a speedier conclusion.

Issue: Saturday, 15th December, 1917.

Entertainment to Wounded Sailors:

On Thursday afternoon the members of the various Girls' Auxiliaries and of the Sphagnum Moss Work Party entertained a party of wounded sailors from Dungavel in the East Church Hall, which was beautifully decorated with ever green and flowers, When the party arrived in motors they were kindly welcomed by their young hostesses, and were soon comfortably seated enjoying the bounteous fare provided for them. Tea over, and tables cleared, games were interspersed with songs by guests and hostesses. Much merriment was caused by the hat-trimming and hair dressing competitions, the winners receiving handsome prizes. Towards the end of the entertainment the thanks of the sailors were voiced by one of their number in a neat speech.

Lanarkshire Volunteers - Strathaven Branch:

A well attended meeting of representative townsmen was held in the Parish Council Chambers on 7th inst., to meet Captains Hastie and Lennox, of the Lanarkshire Territorial Association. It was then unanimously agreed to promote the formation of a Volunteer corps for this district. Mr John S. Duncan, the secretary, assisted by Messrs Wm. Smith and J.J. Barrie will attend at the Parish Council Chambers this evening, and on Tuesday and Saturday evenings next, for the purpose of enrolling members and giving any information desired. While all men over 18 years of age will be welcomed, the appeal to enrol is specially directed to men who are holding certificates of exemption from military serve, and to those over military age. Volunteers can be called out only in case of threatened invasion, and then only for home defence. See advert.

Issue: Saturday, 22nd December, 1917.

The Property Market:

The property known as Greenhill Cottage, belonging to the late Miss Marion Martin was sold by public roup in the Public Hall on Tuesday at the upset price of £850. The assessed rental is £36, and the Feu Duty and stipend amount to £1.5s.5d.

Parish Church Woman's Guild Concert:

On 14th inst., a splendid entertainment was given by the Guild in the Public Hall, on behalf of the Soldiers' Comforts Fund. The first part of the programme was contributed by children under the leadership of Miss Helen Mc Coll. They did their bit with distinction, and held the eager attention of an audience that packed the hall in every part. Resounding applause marked the completion of every succeeding item and this applause was richly deserved. The second part was contributed by adult artistes. Miss Isa Kyle delighted the audience with her very fine voice - every item was encored. Miss Aitken provided a very promising young elocutionist sure to be heard of again. The singing of Sergt. Tuffrey was of a refined and pure tone. He has a fine tenor voice. Lance-Corporal Watson surprised his audience with his extraordinary baritone singing, and both these khaki men had to respond again and again with encores. Mr Hugh McNeilly, bass, sang with great power "Toreador" and "The Old Brigade." He is always a favourite in Strathaven. Mention must be made of Lance-Corporal Jelly, F.R.C.O., who acted as accompanist with great skill and feeling. The Rev. J. Muirhead presided.

Presentation to Mrs Donald Hareshaw:

On Christmas evening, a large number of the friends of Mr and Mrs Donald, Hareshaw, met in the hall of the Crown Hotel, Strathaven, to convey to them the regret of the community on their departure, and to ask them to accept as tokens of respect and good wishes a gold watch and chain for Mr Donald and a timepiece and a diamond and ruby ring for Mrs Donald, together with a wallet of Treasury notes. Mr Thomas Findlay, Drumclog, occupied the chair, and referred to his long acquaintanceship with Mr and Mrs Donald, to the high estimation in which they were held in the district, and to the general regret felt on their retiral from farming. Dr. Watson, in handing over the gifts expressed the feeling that Mr Donald's place would be difficult to fill in the parish, as he had maintained, unblemished, a standard of conduct in his dealings, which were always straight, and honourable, and required no bond for fulfilment. In a feeling reply, Mr Donald thanked the donors for the gifts, which, he said, would be treasured in life and handed down afterwards as heirlooms in the family. On behalf of his wife and family, he thanked the company for the kind references to them, and stated that, like most farmers, it was to his good wife that he owed much of his success in life. He had seen many changes in his time, had his ups and downs like other people, and many a time he would have been quite pleased to retain the wallet of notes, but, as he felt he had no particular need of them, he would like to hand them over to the Royal Scottish Agricultural Benevolent Association. For many years he had taken a great interest in this worthy society, and as the Strathaven district had both subscribed liberally to, and received liberally from, this society, he had much pleasure in handing to Mr John Watson, Kirkwood House, the Lanarkshire secretary of the society, the wallet, which contained £20. Mr Watson, on behalf of the society, in a racy speech, thanks Mr Donald for the gift, and stated the benefit such well-won annuities were to recipients. At present £80 a year came into the parish in this way, and he hoped Mr Donald's example would stimulate others to support such a worthy cause. Mr Robert McCowan proposed "The Town and Trade of the District," and Mr Dalglish replied. Mr W, Dykes, Hazliebank, proposed "Agriculture," and dealt with the extreme necessity of every farmer putting forth his best effort to increase the food supply of the country, and Mr James Young, Greenfield, in reply, homologated all Mr Dykes had to say with regard to economy and food production. Singers were numerous, and a splendid musical programme brought a most enjoyable evening to a close with many and heartfelt wished for the happiness of Mr and Mrs Donald in their retirement.

Hamilton Advertiser

Issue Saturday, 5th January, 1918.

Donaldson Soup Kitchen:

The children attending the Soup Kitchen had the usual special treats this year. On Christmas Day, Mr and Mrs John Baird of Colinhill provided each child with sweets, cracker and picture book, and on New Year's Day, following a long established custom, pies were given, provided for by one gift of a sheep from Mr Murray of Stromolloch. The portions of the sheep not utilised were distributed among the older poorer people of the town, an extension of the gift greatly appreciated by all the recipients. The committee of the Soup Kitchen desire to return their sincere thanks to the donors of these gifts and also to Mr Francis Lambie of Roundhill for a very generous supply of potatoes and turnips. Subscriptions for the useful agency may be given to Mr John Torrance or to any of the local ministers.

Rankin U.F. Church Sunday School:

There was a splendid attendance of children on Thursday evening in the hall of the church, at the Sunday School party - from little tots on the Cradle Roll to those whose ideas are soaring in the direction of the Bible class. After a modest tea, games were heartily engaged in, with quieter intervals between, when instrumental music, recitations, and songs were contributed by scholars: a particularly pleasing feature being the rendering of some of the action hymns which Miss Taylor and her staff of young teachers have taught to the children of the primary departments. Prizes were presented to those who had attended with perfect regularity during the year, including a Bible presented to Miss Jeanie Millar for ten years perfect attendance. A very happy time ended with a visit from Santa Claus who bestowed on everybody present a gift, provided by enthusiastic teachers and their friends.

Strathaven Calendars:

War conditions, scarcity of paper etc., and the consequent high prices had the effect of reducing materially the number of calendars issued at this time, but the well known firm of R Thomson, family grocer, 1 Townhead Street, has adhered to the annual custom . . . . .

War Fund Operetta - "The Magic Ruby":

They don't do things by halves in Strathaven when it comes to running a kinderspiel - at least that's the experience of the writer who has during the last 3 years witnessed performances all having for their subject the augmentation of the lead war relief funds. Last Saturday evening the first of 4 performances was given of the oriental operetta, in 3 acts, entitled "The Magic Ruby," a stone which is connected with the fortunes of a young Government clerk and his fiance and how the magic ruby of the Rajah of Rajahpore disappeared and was ultimately recovered.

Issue: Saturday, 12th January, 1918.

War Work Party:

Mrs Lee Dykes begs to acknowledge with many thanks the sum of £1 collected by Miss Lily Elder and Miss Nance Stewart, from the sale of lavender bags.

Seasonable Benevolence:

Through the kindness of Mr and Mrs Lee Dykes of Overton, the old folks tea was given as usual this year in the Cinema House. It is a kind and good work, and greatly appreciated and enjoyed by the guests, who were not slow to show their gratitude.

Strathaven Branch, B.W.T.A:

The monthly members' meeting took place in the Mission Hall on Wednesday afternoon. Mrs McRorie ably presided, and the speaker was Mrs Dey, who gave many interesting details of her work among the soldiers in France. Mrs J Bryson presided at the harmonium, Miss Bryson sang two beautiful solos, while her two little brothers gave three recitations very cleverly. Tea was served as usual.

The Day of Thanksgiving and Prayer:

The Day of Thanksgiving and Prayer was observed in all the churches in the town on Sabbath, and in the evening there was a united service in the Public Hall. There was a full attendance. The Rev. James McRorie presided, and the Rev. M.U. Baird and the Rev. T.M. Dey read the lessons and engaged in devotional exercises. The address was given by the Rev. John Muirhead, who chose as his subject, 2nd Chronicles xx., 13, "The Valley of Blessing," dividing it under these heads:- (1) A nation appearing before God; (2) God on the side of the nation: (3) The nation blessing God in the valley of Berachah, and applying it to the present need. The collection was on behalf of the War Relief Fund.

Parish Council of Avondale:

The monthly meeting was held on Tuesday. Present - Messrs Andrew Barr, W.R. Brown, R.R. Galloway, John Hamilton, James Lindsay, Robert Mitchell, John Wiseman, William Wright, Patrick Wynn, and William Dykes (chairman). A recommendation by the Works Committee, as to the purchase of land at Holm Street, at a sum not exceeding £50 be offered the s of Mr Galloway for the land. Mr Lindsay moved that the recommendation be not approved. This was not seconded, and Mr Wiseman's motion was carried. Mr Cameron, C.C., attended during the hearing of appeals against payment of rates, all being relieved. It was unanimously agreed to provide further ground for garden plots, and the Clerk was instructed to let the southern part of the Hastie Park on the same terms as the other plots. Poor Law cases were considered, and accounts amounted to £245.0s.5d passed for payment.

Meatless Day:

From advert it will be seen that the local butchers have agreed to close every Wednesday as a meatless day. It is hoped the public will assist them as far as possible in not taking extra supply of meat on Tuesdays or other days.

Cadets:

A company of the 1st Lanarkshire Battalion has now been formed at the Academy under the instruction of Mr Munro. All youths between the ages of 13 and 18 are eligible to join, and already forty have enrolled. The drill is held on Friday nights in the Central Hall of the Academy. Last Friday Major Hamilton, Rutherglen, officer commanding the battalion, visited the company, and gave an interesting lecture on the value of Cadet training, and then took the company for drill. It is hoped that more young people will come forward to enrol and get the benefit of Cadet military training.

Save the Children:

The Scottish Band of Hope Union, whose motto is "Save the Children," offered to give book prizes for the best essays written in school on "Alcohol and Health," which was the subject of lecture by their agent, Mr Robert Crosbie, on his annual visit to the Academy on 31st October, 1917. The results are now announced, and the following have been awarded prizes:- Higher Grade Department - Jessie Barr, Wm. Miller. Jeanie A.S. Park, James Law, and A. Thomson Wilson. Supplementary Department - Nessie Barclay, Margaret Kyle, and Wm. C. Millar. Senior Department - Ina Miller, Chrissie Gilmour, Wm. Tennent, Wm. Chapman, Jessie Park, John M. Bryson, and Charles Wilson.

Mutual Improvement Association:

The meetings of this association were resumed on Monday night after its Christmas recess, when the Rev. Mr Baird gave a paper entitled "A Naval Base and its People." As Mr Baird had spent four months at Rosyth base last summer, those who braved the elements were well rewarded by getting a glimpse of a part of Scotland which, hitherto stagnant, is now rapidly being transformed into a busy hive of industry. Mr Baird traced the rise of the British fleet from the reign of James 1 when the bold Sir Andrew Wood defeated the English and has, as a base for his ships, a port in the Firth of Forth. Now this is the very area which the Admiralty has selected as a base for part of the Grand Fleet. In the centre of the dockyards stands Rosyth Castle, which has been preserved through all these years. The two other outstanding objects of interest are the Commander -in-Chief's office, with its wireless station and the oil tanks. The population is very varied - Aberdonians, Cockneys, English, Welsh, and Scotch-Canadians being massed together. The lecturer then gave a description of the Garden City of Rosyth, which is being built at present, and is attached to the dockyard. There is no doubt but that Scotland will gain much by the establishment of this great naval base.

Issue: Saturday, 26th January, 1918.

Avondale War Relief Fund:

The local Boy Scouts are organising a collection of scrap metal, bottles and waste paper throughout Strathaven and district, the proceeds to be devoted towards the local War Relief Fund. For the purpose of the collection the town is being divided into districts, and leaflets will shortly be distributed advising householders when the collection is to be taken in their particular area.

Surprisingly large sums have already been raised in other towns by this method, and it is confidently expected that a similar result will be attained in Strathaven.

Mutual Improvement Association:

On Monday evening there was a good attendance at the weekly meeting, when Mr John Watson, Glasgow, delivered a paper entitled "Some Phases of Burns." Mr Watt, in a few words, introduced the speaker, who gave a brief resume of the poet's life - his early education, his father's death and Burns' untimely burden of sorrow and care. Judging, he said, by the literature Burns read, he was fairly well equipped for life's burdens. His poems were true picture of Scottish peasant life, and surely no one was in a better position to portray this life than Burns himself, to whom we are indebted for the preservation of the Scottish Doric. The address was interspersed with suitable quotations from the poet's works, and a very hearty vote of thanks to the lecturer manifested the appreciation of the audience.

Soldiers' and Sailors' Parcels:

Acknowledgments are now coming to hand from the recipients of the parcels despatched last week by the Rankin United Free Church to those connected with the congregation who are serving in the Army and Navy. A special collection for this object realised £145.9s.3d; by the sale of artificial flowers, made by a willing and busy band of workers, more than £11 were realised; a young lady obtained £1 as the result of her enterprise on Hallowe'en night; while the sum of £3.9s was handed in from the sale of photographs of the Rev. T. M. Dey and Mrs Dey, in their uniforms as Y.M.C.A. workers. Mr William Blake and Mr S.W. Gilmour gave special gifts, and children contributed their quota. With the total sum of £32.5s thus provided, excellent parcels were sent to sixty-six men. The replies that are coming in show how highly they appreciate the gifts, and how glad they are to know that those at home remember them.

Issue: Saturday, 2nd March, 1918.

Picture House:

We note that the manager of our local Picture House has been able to secure the splendid 4,000 feet picture "Florence Nightingale" ("The Lady of the Lamp") for next week. A splendid variety programme is also advertised for tonight - For particulars see advertisement.

Sphagnum Moss Dressings:

The work of making these dressings is being pursued with great zeal by the ladies who meet in the Rankin Church Hall every Thursday afternoon and evening. An intimation from overseas has been received *"which makes it apparent that moss dressings will in future be used to a much greater extent than formerly, their value as a dressing, and as a substitute for cotton wool, having bee4n definitely recognised."* The ladies in charge of this work would welcome many additional helpers, so that the weekly output of dressings may be very largely increased.

War Relief Fund:

As the result of the performance of the operetta, "The Magic Ruby," in the Public Hall here, the sum of £40 has been handed to the Relief Funds, one half to the Strathaven Work Party and one half to the general War Fund. The committee, Messrs W.R. Wilson (convener), Wm. Brown, Robert Leggate, James McIlveen, James C. Stewart, and J.P. Morrison (secretary), are to be congratulated on this handsome result from the immense amount of time and personal trouble they devoted to secure this pronounced success in every respect.

Mutual Improvement Association:

On Monday evening the concluding lecture for the session was given by the Rev. T.M. Dey, who had chosen as his subject; "Bits of France." Mr Dey was stationed at Boulogne for four months, and he gave an interesting pictorial description of the town before proceeding to tell about his work. Miscellaneous duties fall to the Y.M.C.A. worker, but Mr Dey entered into the work with the true spirit, as his paper showed. He explained the different ways in which amusements and recreation were provided for the troops. Competitions, games, lectures and concert parties were arranged for each night in the week, and were all enjoyed by the troops. The hearty vote of thanks which was accorded the lecturer manifested the appreciation of the audience.

Dungavel Royal Naval Hospital Patients:

With the object of entertaining the patients of the Royal Naval Hospital at Dungavel, the Choral Union held two whist drives recently from which a sufficient sum was realised. The entertainment came off in the East U.F. Church Hall on Wednesday last. The men arrived punctually at 2.30 p.m. and were welcomed by the committee of ladies. After doing justice to a sumptuous tea, the "Grand Old Duke of York" put the company into a free and happy mood. Prizes were given for the following competitions: hat trimming, drawing, singing, and potato race. All the competitions were entered into with zest, and caused great merriment. Time passed all too quickly, and after a second tea one of the patients called for a vote of thanks to the ladies for their kindness in providing such a treat, which was heartily given. After the singing of "Rule Britannia," "Auld Lang Syne," and "God Save the King," the party left for Dungavel at 7.30 p.m, delighted with their afternoon outing.

Issue: Saturday, 9th March, 1918.

Sudden Death:

While on his way to the station on Wednesday morning, Mr John Martin, Douglasdale, Strathaven, dropped dead on Lethame Road. Deceased was formerly employed as a gardener at Dungavel.

L.O.G.T:

The weekly meeting was held in the Good Templars' Hall, Bridge Street, on Monday evening - Sister Moffat, C.T. presiding. The programme provided by the Chief Templar, consisted of gramophone selections, which were thoroughly enjoyed. Bro. Sergeant James M. Bryson, who was home on leave after two years' active service, gave a short address, which was much appreciated.

War Cookery:

Under the auspices of the School Board and the local Food Control Committee, a series of demonstrations in economical cookery will be given by Miss Kathleen P. Young, county instructress, Colinhill School, commencing on Thursday first. It is hoped that, looking to the urgent need for economy in food consumption, these demonstrations will be well attended. For particulars see advert.

Issue: Saturday, 23 March, 1918.

Volunteers:

As will be seen from our advertising columns today, the first meeting of the Strathaven detachment of the Volunteers will be held in the Academy on Wednesday evening. All men from 17 to 60 are invited to enrol for home defence. The men will be supplied with uniforms, rifles and other equipment immediately on enrolment. Men over military age are specially needed in order to set free more men for active service abroad.

Death of Well-Known Avondale Proprietor:

We regret to record the death of Mr Alex. Park, of South Torfoot, which took place on Sunday 17th inst. Mr Park, who came from Sorn about 37 years ago and bought South Torfoot, was one of the best known men in Upper Avondale. A splendid type of the farmer proprietor, he was distinguished for his uprightness and integrity of character, and was greatly beloved by all in the district. A keen Churchman, he was one of a little band of earnest men who determined to raise a church - a suitable memorial to the Covenanters who fought at Drumclog - and no one laboured more earnestly than he to attain this end. He rejoiced greatly when in 1912, the beautiful edifice was opened for public worship, and it remains a lasting memorial to the zeal and self-sacrifice of such as he. For fourteen years he was an elder of the Church of Scotland and, from the beginning, Superintendent of Drumclog Memorial Kirk Sabbath School till failing health compelled him reluctantly to relinquish that office. Mr Park has been in weak health for some time, but last week influenza brought an attack of heart-failure to which he succumbed. He was buried on Wednesday last in Strathaven Cemetery - a very large company of mourners following his remains to their last resting place. He is survived by a widow and two daughters.

Issue: Saturday 30th March, 1918

Tennis Club:

The Annual General Meeting was held in the clubhouse last Saturday afternoon - the president, Mr Wm. Allan, presiding. There was a fair turnout of members present. The secretary and treasurer, Mr Robert Park, submitted his financial report which showed a good credit balance. It was decided to get a few repairs made to the clubhouse and netting, and to open the courts on the first Saturday of May.

Volunteers:

The first muster of the Strathaven section of the 2/1st Battalion of the Lanarkshire Volunteer Regiment took place in the Academy on Wednesday evening. Lieutenant Smellie, Hamilton, and a number of non-com officers were present and gave full explanations. Twenty-five men were enrolled. Drilling will commence on Wednesday, 3rd prox, when further enrolments can be made. It is hoped that the section will be considerably augmented particularly by the men engaged in agriculture, and that all intending to volunteer will do so immediately. It should be kept in view that men of all medical grades are eligible, provided they pass an examination by the local medical officer.

Issue: Saturday, 6th April, 1918.

The Late Miss Elizabeth Giffen - Important Public Bequests:

In the passing away of Miss Elizabeth Giffen, Blackwood, Kirk Street, Strathaven has lost a gentlewoman of a type that in this busy, bustling, hurrying age is fast disappearing. Quiet in manner, unobtrusive, observant, deeply interested in the welfare of her friends and neighbours, and fond of reminiscent talk upon former days and ways in Avondale, she lived her almost four score years wisely and usefully unknown to fame. That was reserved for her distinguished brother Sir Robert Giffen, LL.D., K.C.B., of whose solid achievements in the world of finance and literature connected therewith, she was naturally and justly proud. With her another family history ends that shows what Scottish grit and energy and ability can accomplish. Under her Deed of Settlement, Miss Giffen, after making some personal bequests, and providing legacies free of duty of £100 to the East U.F. Church for the poor of the congregation, £100 to the Parish Council for the other poor of the parish, £22 and bed linen to the District Nursing Association, and a selection of her books to the Mutual Improvement Association, has left the bulk of her estate for providing a Cottage Hospital for residenters in the parish of Avondale.

The residue of here estate will amount to about £1300 plus the value of the deceased's cottage and furniture (after writing down the value of several railway investments to present day values).

Issue: Saturday, 13th April, 1918.

Strathaven and the War:

News has come to hand of the death of Lieutenant William Watt of the Lancashire Fusiliers, son of Mr Robert Watt, Greenwoodbank, Overton Road. After distinguishing himself in the recent fighting, he was seriously wounded in the left thigh, and brought over to a London hospital, where the wound proved to be fatal. Private Peter McCallum, Kirk Street, has been killed in action. He was a butcher to trade.

Ticket-of-Leave - Man's Omission:

Having been liberated on licence from Peterhead Prison on 2nd January from a sentence of three years' penal servitude for housebreaking with previous convictions, Robert Wilson, labourer, lately residing at Castle Street, Strathaven, pled guilty before Hon. Sheriff Stodart at Hamilton on Monday to the charge of failing to report to the authorities his arrival at Strathaven on 3rd January, and his change of address from there to Coalburn on 8th January. He was sentenced to thirty days imprisonment.

Farm Servants' Union:

A meeting of the Strathaven branch of the Scottish Farm Servants' Union was held in the Lesser Public Hall on Sunday last. Mr J. Currie, president of the branch presided over a good attendance. Addresses were delivered by Mr John Anthony, Renfrew, and Mr George Coupland, organiser, Lanark, both of whom dealt at considerable length with the need for union amongst agricultural workers, and the benefits to be derived therefrom. It was resolved that the rate of increase - 6s per week - which had been obtained in Lanark district, also be asked for Strathaven district. A number of members were enrolled at the close.

School Board:

The usual monthly meeting was held in the Board Room on Tuesday last, Dr. Mason, chairman, presided. Two defaulters were summoned before the Board for failure to send their children regularly to school, and promised amendment. The clerk reported that the case of one parent had been dealt with by the Sheriff, and had been continued meantime to see whether any improvement had taken place in the children's record of attendance. One application for exemption from school attendance was left over for consideration at next meeting. A letter from Father O'Leary was read resigning his position as a member of the Board owing to his departure from Strathaven. The appointment of a member to fill the vacancy was meantime held over.

Parish Council of Avondale:

The monthly meeting was held on Tuesday all the members being present - Mr William Dykes in the chair. Intimation was read from Messrs J & J Barrie, writers, that the late Miss Giffen, Blackwood

Cottage, Kirk Street, had bequeathed £100 to the Parish Council, the interest to be distributed annually to the poor. The council cordially accepted this trust, and also recorded their high appreciation that Miss Giffen had left the residue of her estate to such a worthy public object as a Cottage Hospital. It was decided to grant an additional bonus of £10 per annum to Mr A. Wilson, clerk, and £5 bonus to Miss Wilson, assistant, both from February 15th. Applications for the situation of park ranger, etc., having been submitted, Mr Joseph Hamilton was appointed. Poor Law matters and finance were then considered, accounts amounting to £383.8s.4d being passed for payment.

Issue: Saturday, 20th April, 1918.

Barnock Public School War Savings Association:

During War Weapons Week Barnock Public School collected £240.9s - enough to provide three machine guns. It is a small association, the number at school being only 22, so the result is considered very satisfactory.

Strathaven Academy - War Weapons Week:

The amount subscribed by the pupils of Strathaven Academy reached the sum of £242. 6s.6d which is sufficient to purchase 3 machine guns. The total now collected by the School War Savings Association is £1243.

Military Funeral:

On Monday last the remains of Lieutenant William Watt, Lancashire Fusiliers, only son of Mr Robert Watt, Greenwoodbank, Overton Road, were laid to rest in the Strathaven Cemetery. The funeral was of a semi-military character, there being six privates, one corporal, and one piper present. The coffin was covered with the Union Jack, and by a large number of wreaths which had been sent by his comrades and friends. The procession wended its way to the cemetery, the piper playing, "The Flowers of the Forest." Arriving at the cemetery the coffin was carried shoulder high from the hearse to the grave by the military party. Prayers having been offered, the piper played the funeral dirge, after which the bugler sounded "The Last Post." The funeral was largely attended by all classes of the community and large crowds assembled on the route and at the cemetery to witness the proceedings. The following took part in the service - Rev. J. Muirhead, B.D., Strathaven, Rev. William Thomson, Chapelton; and Rev. N. R. Noble, Cambuslang. The following letter was received by the deceased's father:-

"France, March 28th, 1918. Dear Mr Watt - You will have had a War Office telegram that your son was wounded on the 26th. I met him as he was being carried out. He appeared to me to be seriously wounded, but I am inclined to hope, not dangerously. I think it was only his thigh that was affected. If so (and the artery did not appear to be damaged), then he would certainly recover after a month or so in hospital. He is a very great loss to me and to the battalion, being quite one of my best and most gallant subalterns, and very much loved by his men. I trust that his wound may be quickly got in hand, and that safely out of this, you may have the pleasure of seeing him before long. Excuse a hasty letter, but you will know the conditions under which I write - Yours sincerely P.T. Croley, Lt. Colonel Canada with Lancashire Fusiliers."

Issue: Saturday, 27th April, 1918.

Prohibition Rally:

Under the auspices of the British Women's Temperance Association, a meeting in connection with the prohibition campaign was held in the Town Hall on Tuesday evening last. The Rev. James

McRorie presided, and was accompanied on the platform by the president, Mrs Lusk, Mrs McRorie, and the Rev. M. U. Baird. Rev. D. H. Gerrard, Councillor Cameron, Mr James Millar, Dr. Watt and Mr N. W. Bryson. There was a large and representative attendance. The Rev. W. D. Miller, of Ruchill, Glasgow, was the first speaker, and dealt in a vigorous manner with the question of prohibition in its relation to the good of the people, the carrying on of the war, and the moral well-being of the nation. He blamed the Government for having neither courage nor foresight in their treatment of this question. The "Women's Vote" was the subject of a bright, happy, and informing speech from Mrs Sommerville Smith, of Glasgow. She urged that now that the vote had been secured, it must be used, and more particularly she urged its use as a "gun in the prohibition offensive." A resolution, "Respectfully urging the Government to prohibit the sale of intoxicating liquor," was moved by the Rev. M. U. Baird, seconded by Mr N. W. Bryson, and passed unanimously. During the evening a large choir, under the leadership of Mr David Hamilton, organist of the East Church, charmed the audience with their splendid singing, and acceptable solos were rendered by Miss A. Brownlie and Mr A. C. Hilston. After the customary vote of thanks, the meeting closed with the singing of the National Anthem.

The Late Mrs Donaldson:

The funeral of Mrs Donaldson, wife of the Rev. Alex. W. Donaldson, B.A., senior minister of the East Church, took place to Strathaven Cemetery on Tuesday of this week. A short service was held in the East Church, and the large attendance testified to the esteem in which Mrs Donaldson was held, and the sympathy felt with her husband in his bereavement. At the close of the service on Sabbath last, the Rev. Matthew Urie Baird, M.A., made the following reference-" *It will be your desire that I should make a brief reference to the loss that we, as a congregation, have sustained in the death of Mrs Donaldson. With tragic suddenness the blow has fallen. Though not perhaps in her usual robust health lately, Mrs Donaldson had been going about her ordinary pursuits, and on Sabbath last, as her custom was, she was at church at both services. Contracting a chill, pneumonia intervened, and she died early on Friday evening. Of Mrs Donaldson it is hardly necessary to speak. Your won hearts bear her witness. We remember with gratitude her deep devotion to her husband, and her strong and unfailing support of him in all his work, her abounding hospitality, her quiet, unselfish, and untiring interest in the work of Christ's Kingdom, not only in this church, but in the Church at large, and her many remembered, but little known acts of kindness and of love. As one of those women who minister unto Him, she has entered into the joy and peace of the Master's Home. Our beloved senior minister had had much sorrow, but he has great faith - tried often, always strong. Our hearts go out to him in deepest sympathy, love, and affection in this deep sorrow. To him, to Miss Brown, and to the sorrow circle we can but express our sorrow and sympathy, and commend them to the grace of God, which is in Christ Jesus our Lord."* Numerous floral tributes were an expression of the sympathy expressed so widely and included wreaths from the East Church Session and East Church Sabbath School.

West Church Wedding:

Considerable interest was aroused on Friday last by a marriage which took place in the West U.F. Church. It is sometime since a church wedding was held here, so quite a large audience collected to witness the ceremony conducted by the Rev. James McRorie. The bride, Miss J. Mcilwain, looked charming in her bridal dress of pure white, while the bridegroom, Mr John Green, who is an S.B.A. at Dungavel Royal Naval Hospital, looked very smart in his blue uniform. After the ceremony, the bride and bridegroom passed from the church under the flags of the Allies, held by some of the convalescent patients from the hospital, and proceeded to walk to the Town Hall, where a reception of guests was held.

Second Lieutenant John M. Hood:

Mr James Hood, Dunlop Street, has been officially notified that his son, Second-Lieu., John M. Hood, has been missing since the 24th of July.

"Shoogly Brig":

"My attention has been called to a paragraph appearing in "The Handbook of Strathaven," page 41, where it says that the "Shoogly Brig" is a favourite spot for picnics. The proprietors wish me to make it known that this ground is private property, and owing to the abuse made by picnic parties, the privilege has been withdrawn - **N.W. Bryson, Townhead Street.**"

Issue: Saturday, 11th May, 1918.

"Shoogly Brig":

It was stated in error in last Saturday's "Advertiser" that the privilege of walking over the grass lands of Primrose Braes (South Newton) had been withdrawn, as proprietors had never been asked for leave nor granted it.

Croix De Guerre:

The many friends of William Watson, B.Sc., youngest son of our esteemed road surveyor, will be pleased to learn that he has had the honour of having the Croix De Guerre conferred upon him by the French Government, for services on the field. Corporal Watson enlisted in the Gordon's, and was transferred to the Royal Engineers. His three brothers are all in His Majesty's forces - the eldest, Peter, has been a prisoner in Germany since 1914.

Boys' Brigade:

On Wednesday evening, the local company of the Boys' Brigade had a special turnout, which took the form of a route march. The procession was led by pipers Arch. Johnstone and Wm. Binnie, and after circulating the town they went to Glassford and back. The present company of the Boys' Brigade is of very recent institution in the town, and the alert appearance of the boys in their smart uniform reflects much credit on the leaders, Capt. J. Johnstone, and Lieut., G. McCallum.

Issue: Saturday, 18th May, 1918.

Distinguished Conduct Medal:

Last week we announced that Corporal Wm. Watson had been awarded the Croix De Gueere. This week we are pleased to learn the British Government have conferred on him the Distinguished Conduct Medal for services in the field.

Military Medallist:

News has been received by Mr John Leggate, 44 Ballgreen, Strathaven, that his eldest son, Robert, Black Watch, has been awarded the Military Medal for work done on the field in the last big push. Before enlisting Private Leggate was an attendant at Lanarkshire District Asylum, Hartwood, and previous to that worked as a butcher with Mr Wm. Watt, Townhead Street, Strathaven. He is married, and his wife resides at South Uist.

An Obstreperous Farm Servant:

Yesterday, at Hamilton Sheriff Court, Wm. Hood, Farm Servant, Kirkwood Farm, Strathaven, pled guilty to the following three charges, viz., (1) on 16th May he committed a breach of the peace at Drumclog Public House, Todshill Street, (2) in said public-house he maliciously broke the glass of two pictures, (3) in Kirk Street, on same date, he assaulted Police Sergeant William McLeach, while the latter was engaged in the execution of his duty. A fine of £2 or ten days was imposed.

Issue: Saturday, 25th May, 1918.

A Tribute to Scottish Music:

Lady Margaret Scott, eldest daughter of the Duke of Buccleuch, who has been doing noble national work at the front, has accepted the dedication of a Scotch Mazurka, "Scots in Poland,"

By Dr. Machardy, and wishes him success in his endeavour to popularise our country's music.

Help our Prisoners of War:

The band (33 performers) of the Depot, the Cameronians, Scottish Rifles, (Lieut. Colonel C.B. Vandeleur, commanding, visits Strathaven today to assist in raising funds for the relief of Strathaven's prisoners of war. The Strathaven Academy Company of the 1st Lanarkshire Cadet Battalion, the Strathaven Boys' Brigade, and the Strathaven Boy Scouts, will parade the town in uniform. A splendid programme will be given by the band in the George Allan Public Park bandstand in the evening. See advert.

Military Cross:

Mr J.G. Greenshields Leadbetter, younger, of Stobieside, has been awarded the Military Cross. He received the commission in the Lanarkshire Yeomanry in January 1914, and is now a captain in that regiment, with which he served in Gallipoli, Egypt and Sinai. For some time he has been seconded to the Machine Gun Corps, and it was for service with this corps that the cross was gained. His action is thus officially described - *"For having on March 27th, at Amman, after reconnoitring well forward, got his section into action 1,500 yards from the enemy position, and provided a covering fire which saved us many casualties as our advance developed."* Mr Greenshields Leadbetter has been in Palestine during all the operation there. He was educated at Ardvreck, and Rugby, and at Ch. Ch., Oxford, from which college he received his B.A. in absence on active service.

Issue: Saturday, 1st June, 1918.

The Golf Course:

The course is now in good condition, and householders should recommend it to visitors as the best and most enjoyable way of spending their holiday.

Dr. Machardy:

Dr. Machardy, while cycling, was overtaken by a motorist last Monday, knocked down, and his cycle wrecked. He was to have given a Scottish Concert on 3rd June, but it has been postponed until his recovery from the injuries he received.

Red Cross Concert at Sandford:

In aid of the Red Cross, a very enjoyable and successful little concert by the school children, organised by Miss Barr, the headmistress, assisted by Miss Hamilton, the assistant teacher, took place on Wednesday night of last week, before an audience which crowded the old schoolroom. Mr Shearer, chairman of the Board, presided, and in explaining the object for which the concert was held, made reference to the beneficent work of the Red Cross, and the gratification it gave to have these little contributions from time to time from the children of Sandford. The programme which consisted of songs, recitations, and dialogues, was very creditably rendered by the children and was greatly enriched by contributions from Mr and Mrs Martin. The sum of £5.12s.6d on this occasion was collected.

Issue: Saturday, 15th June, 1918.

Presentation:

On Tuesday evening, the Rev. James McRorie, minister of the West Church; Dr. Alan Watt, preses; and Mr John Russell, representing the office-bearers, Sabbath School teachers and friends in the congregation, handed over in their name to Mr Adam Grierson, at his home at Muirbank, a framed photograph and a rest chair, as a tangible token of the great respect and high esteem in which he is held by them. The photograph bears the following inscription: *"Presented to Mr Adam Grierson, along with a rest chair, as a token of appreciation of his valuable services to the West Church, Strathaven, as preses, manager, and Sabbath School teacher, and for 30 years as elder and superintendent of the Sabbath School, June, 1918."* A duplicate of the photograph is hung in the vestry. At the same time, the opportunity was taken of presenting Mrs Grierson with a pair of silver candlesticks. Mrs Grierson has taught in the Sabbath School for 33 years. Mr Grierson for 40 years, and Miss Muir, his sister-in-law, for 60 years - a total of 133 years - an honourable family record of Christian service in Sabbath School work.

Issue: Saturday, 22 June, 1918.

A Farmer's Offence:

On Thursday, in Hamilton Sheriff Court, an Avondale farmer was charged with having ill-treated and over-drawn a brown mare yoked to a spring cart, and with having driven recklessly to the danger of the lieges. Mr P.R. Soutter, writer, Hamilton, tendered a plea of guilty subject to an explanation in extenuation. A person, he said, was quite entitled to punish a horse that was restive, and in this case the question of punishment was one of degree, the respondent claiming that he had not excessively punished the mare. He also held that he had full control of the animal, and would have drawn-up when required. A fine of 30/- with the option of 8 days imprisonment, was imposed.

Issue: Saturday, 29th June, 1918.

Drumclog Scholars' BTT:

During Red Cross Week, the sum of £8.10s was collected by the scholars of Drumclog Public School.

Flag Day:

The Flag Day today is for the orphans of soldiers and sailors of the Lanark Hospital. It is hoped everyone will give generously to this good cause. See advert.

Presentation to Mr Andrew Leiper, Cloverhill:

Mr Leiper having left Cloverhill to take over the farm at Midbrackenridge, has given up supplying his customers in the districts of Tollcross and Parkhead, Glasgow. To mark the occasion of his going to another farm, and after 40 years on the road, his customers in the above districts presented him last week, with a handsome pocket book, and a beautiful handbag for his good lady, Mrs Leiper. It is not often that one's customers are so generous, but Mr Leiper's kind and genial manner could not go unrecognised, and the suggestion of a presentation to him was eagerly taken up and willingly subscribed to. The presentation was made by Mrs Buchanan of 'Auchenshaw, Tollcross, who, in the name of the subscribers, wished Mr and Mrs Leiper long life and prosperity in their new home.

Issue: Saturday, 14 June, 1918.

Miss Baxter left on Monday to undertake war work under the Army Medical Board.

Issue: Saturday, 6th July, 1918.

Gilmourton Sabbath School:

The children of this school had their usual outing on Saturday last, on the invitation of Mrs Morton, they spent a most enjoyable day at East Dykes. The thoughtfulness and kindness of Mrs Morton and family were shown in many ways, and contributed very much to the great success of the picnic.

Rankin United Free Church:

On the invitation of Mr and Mrs Dunlop, the Sabbath School trip took place on Wednesday afternoon to Netherfield Farm. Through the kindness of Mr Stewart (Whinknowe), Mr Dunlop (Netherfield), and Mr Hamilton (Goodsburn), the younger children were conveyed to and from the farm in vans, while great kindness was also shown by Mr Taylor, baker. After a meal of milk and pies on arriving, the children had full scope in the farm field to indulge in games and races - the river also proving an added attraction. Later in the day the parents and teachers were entertained to a hearty tea, which was generously provided by Mr and Mrs Dunlop. Cheers for the host and hostess for their kindness, and for the Rev. D. H. Gerrard for his presence, brought a most enjoyable day to a close.

Parish Council of Avondale:

The monthly meeting was held on Tuesday. Present - Messrs. Andrew Barr, Wm. Beveridge, Wm. R. Brown, R. R. Galloway, John Wiseman, Patrick Wynn, Wm. Wright, and Wm. Dykes, chairman. Request for use of the George Allan Public Park for Red Cross fete etc., having been considered, and a deputation from the fete committee heard, the Council unanimously granted permission as requested - the park to be closed on Saturday, 13th July, except on payment of admission; other days open to the public (collections to be taken if wished), and all entertainments to stop at 10 p.m. daily. The School Board intimated that they required the sum of £2,500 from the rates this year, and increase of £150. The rates for 1918-19 were fixed. The works committee are to report as to site, etc., of suggested children's yacht pond in Hastie Park. Poor Law cases were settled and accounts (£193.0s.10d) passed for payment.

Strathaven Academy - Closing Day:

On Friday, the 28th ult., the pupils of all the departments of the school assembled in the Central Hall - Dr. Mason, chairman of the Avondale School Board, presiding. Owing to the continuance of war conditions, no prizes were given save those mentioned below. The headmaster reported that the highest possible grants had been earned in all the sections of the school. . . The gold medals, annually presented by Lady Giffen and Dr. Mason, to the dux boy and girl of the school respectively, were won by David F. Anderson and Effie C. Riddell, John Bertram and Cathy

Hyslop ranking second. Mr. Barrie's prizes for proficiency in Latin were awarded to David F. Anderson, Effie C. Riddell, Robert Young, Robert Kyle, and Jenny Miller. It was further reported that the pupils' war savings investments had reached £1,514. And that the various war relief collections for the session amounted to almost £48. The gracious message of Their Majesties the King and Queen to school authorities, teachers, and scholars was read by the headmaster.

Scottish Farm Servants' Union:

A meeting of the above Union was held in the Victoria Hall, Strathaven, on Saturday evening. Mr James McWhirr, president of the local branch, presided over a large attendance. The speaker was Mr G. A. Coupland, local organiser of the Union, who said he wanted specially to appeal to the female farm workers (married and single) to organise, and enumerated the benefits they would derive from membership of the Union, which was a safeguard and would have prevented the muddle of the comb-out, which was caused purely through lack of organisation amongst both farmers and farm servants. He fully reported on the annual meeting held at Pentland on 22nd ult., to which he was a delegate for South Lanark and Peebles. He pointed out the difficulty the Union leaders experience in looking after the interests of a body of workers which was will badly organised, and appealed to every member present to make a point of securing at least one new member each for the next six months. A number of new members were enrolled at the close of the meeting. The following office-bearers were elected for the ensuing six months:- President, Mr James Cartie; secretary, Mr Alex. Cameron; committee - Misses Jean Fleming, Todscastle Farm; Annie Muldoon, Westhouse, Strathaven; Jean McInnes, Low Sunrigg, Stonehouse; Annie Kelly, High Bent, Strathaven; Messrs Harry Anderson, Skeoch, East Kilbride; Archibald Fleming, Bankend, Darvel; Geo. Stewart, Avonbank, Strathaven; Angus McKenzie, Redding, Strathaven.

Issue: Saturday, 13th July, 1918.

The Operetta Company:

The Operetta Company have been very busy the last few weeks arranging for the great week of concerts, fairs, and sports, and there is no doubt it will be a great success. See advert.

Scottish Concert:

Dr. Machardy gives a Scottish concert in Strathaven on Thursday of vocal and instrumental arrangements. The programme is a specially fine one, and should attract a large audience.

Issue: Saturday, 20th July, 1918.

The Late Joseph Brown:

One of the best known and most esteemed inhabitants of Strathaven passed away on Wednesday, 10th inst., in the person of Joseph Brown, who for over 39 years has been the church officer of Avondale Parish Church. Seldom has there been a servant of the church who has so worthily discharged the duties of this office over so long a period, and at the same time so as to win and retain the high esteem and respect of all to life's end. "Joseph" was most deservedly beloved by all who knew him, as a man of irreproachable character and rare discretion and judgment. To see him "tak' up the books" on Sunday was an inspiration - a lesson in reverence and devoutness. He was appointed church officer on 27th April, 1879; was ordained to the eldership on 6th October, 1912; and on the 8th July, 1915, the kirk session, on behalf of the congregation, presented him with an illuminated address and a handsome cheque, as a token of their love and esteem. For some months passed he had been in failing health, and on Wednesday, he quietly passed to his rest, aged 85 years. The funeral, which was largely attended, took place on Saturday last to Strathaven cemetery, those officiating being Mr N. W. Bryson, superintendent of the Sabbath School; the Rev. J. Muirhead, B.D., minister of the parish - and the Rev. Wm. Thomson, M.A., minister of Chapelton.

Red Cross Fete:

A fete and fancy fair was held all last week under the management of the Operetta Company in the George Allan Public Park, and was a great success, large crowds being present at all the events, especially was this the case on Monday and Wednesday. The concerts held nightly have been the tit-bit of the event, and the artistes, both local and from other places were of a very high standard. The merry-go-round proved a great attraction for the children, and the sale of donations was also a great success. The tea tent on Saturday was full all afternoon, and under the charge of the lady members of the operetta company did a rousing trade. The whole venture has been a great success, and there is a talk of a ladies' football match being held today. The drawings from Saturday go to the Red Cross fund, and the drawing for the rest of the week to the War Relief Fund.

Issue: Saturday, 27th July, 1918.

War Fund Exposition:

The inhabitants are looking forward with great expectation to the FDP and free gift sale to be held in the West Overton Park on 3rd August. There are a great number of events, including FDP, exhibition of cattle horses, sheep, driving classes, racing, pony trot, decorated lorries etc; also free gift sale of farm and dairy products. See advert.

Scottish Concert:

Dr. Robert Machardy's concert of his arrangements of Scottish music and original works was much enjoyed by an appreciative audience. Miss Baxter sang "British Volunteers and Freedom's Flag" in fine style; Miss Hope displayed much skill in a Scotch mazurka, dedicated to Lady Margaret Scott, daughter to the Duke of Buccleuch, and Prince Charlie fantasia; Miss Bryson, A.B.C.M., was an efficient accompanist, and played a grand rondo and delightful Scotch fantasia; Miss Hamilton, a juvenile, was encored for her clever singing of "John Grumlie." and played "Spinning Wheel with much skill; Miss McLaughlan played a beautiful Scotch waltz with artistic touch; Miss B. McLaughlan sang two songs, displaying a voice of good compass; Miss J. Hamilton, accompanied by Miss Gilchrist, 11 years old, gave a nice rendering of "Duncan Gray"; Mr Jackson, (violin) played, with Dr. Machardy, a fine Scotch duet for piano and violin; Mr Brown was encored for his graphic performance of "The Cuckoo Waltz." Mr Murdoch, a talented boy, sang "The Laird o' Cockpen," and played "Empire Waltz." Dr Machardy's playing and singing received great applause. His Scottish concert was a high-class entertainment, unadulterated by anything German.

Fete Week:

The "Glasgow Fair" week this year has been one complete series of fun and amusement. Never has the town been so full of visitors, and seldom has anything finer been arranged than the fete which was got up entirely by the committee of the Strathaven Operetta Company. The fete commenced on Saturday, 13th July, in the George Allan Public Park.

Issue: Saturday, 10th August, 1918.

Volunteers:

On Wednesday last the local volunteers had shooting practice in a field at West Park Farm.

War Anniversary United Service - A Call to Remembrance:

In commemoration of the fourth anniversary of the declaration of war, a united service of the congregations of the Established and United Free Churches in Strathaven was held on Sunday evening in the Rankin U.F. Church. There was a very large and deeply interested congregation, and the service, which throughout was expressively appropriate for the occasion, was taken part in by the Revs. J. Gilfillan, T. McRorie and J. Muirhead. The two former ministers conducted the opening services and read the Old and New Scripture lessons. The psalms and hymns were also very appropriate, including such grand old tunes as Stroudwater and St. Paul, and the singing, while hearty, was marked by apparent feeling and expression. The Rev. Mr. Muirhead was the preacher. He took for his text, "And thou shall remember all the way which the Lord thy God led thee" (Deuteronomy v111., 2), and in clear, ringing tones delivered a rousing and patriotic sermon that only the day and sacredness of the precincts restrained the congregation from giving audible expression to their appreciation. Deuteronomy, said the preacher, was the book of remembrance, when men who had wandered far from God were recalled to the great things the Lord had done. This glorious faculty of remembrance was what differentiated man from the beasts of the field. Take away memory, and man was to be pitied indeed; and just as memory was to man, so was unity to a nation. They were all proud of being Britons - doubly proud to be Scotchmen - and never so proud as today. They gladly remembered, and it was this remembrance that made them men. Certain things were necessary to be remembered, and it seemed to him that evening, continued the preacher, that the things they were exhorted to remember in this chapter provided him, was an appropriate text for his discourse. They were here called up to acknowledge the goodness of God, and in recalling the past four years of war to remember the day when they were brought out of Egypt. It was on August 4, 1914, that they called in their faculty of remembrance,. It was equally important for them to indulge in the glorious faculty of imagination, and to think what the landing of the Germans on their shores would have meant for them. Think what had happened in Belgium. They had only to bring their recollections and imagination into play to be made ready for every task God had to lay upon them. Yet there were to be found in their midst men who said they were pacifists and conscientious objectors - call them any name you like - but always they were cowards. Mr Muirhead went on to refer to the glorious retreat from Mons, when every man was a hero, and worthy of having his name inscribed on history's roll of fame. Something had happened at the Marne of which he had never heard the true explanation. He could not believe some of the fairy tales about the angels, but whether they believed in angels or not, the fact remained that the Divine Presence was fighting for them, and the angels of God were there to the eye of the seeing and believing soldier, and he was enabled to turn back the hordes of the enemy. People might talk as they liked to-day of this incident, but they would not get any thinking spiritual man that that was not God's hand intervening on the side of justice and truth. Germany had made a terrible blunder in declaring war at the time she did, for had she waited twenty years she would have had a bloodless victory and we would have been her slaves. The preacher went on to say that they were not to provoke the Lord in the wilderness, and to speak of those who again and again murmured against their leaders. Were they less happy or healthy, he asked? No, a little less contented perhaps, but they had never been in hunger; and yet there were men base enough to complain against apparent restrictions on their liberty. Did these men remember those who were fighting for them and the sufferings they endured in the trenches on that first winter of the war? Yet there were those at home who groused about brown bread. It was well for them to recall the way the Lord had led them these last four years in the wilderness, and also to remember that it was God who gave them power to get wealth. They had done so, he was glad to say, the previous day. It was to him one of the grandest sights of their little parish to see men flocking and women serving, all that the boys at the front might be provided with some little comfort and relief. But they were not to rest satisfied with what they had done. There could be no contentment here, so long as men were out there, nor could they pat themselves on the back and think they were jolly good fellows while others continued to fight the nation's battle. *"I pity the miserable creatures,"* said Mr Muirhead, *"who buttons up his pocket after one small donation, and excuses himself from further appeal by imagining he has done his bit. Oh miserable son of God, realise your privilege, and bring your imagination to bear on the situation by thinking of what was taking place in the fair fields of France to-day."* Concluding, Mr Muirhead reminded his hearers that Christ on one occasion had said, *"Do this in remembrance of me."* If they wanted a text to increase their liberality, he gave them these words, and to imagine that they heard some far-off voice asking them to do it in remembrance of what he had done at this time of great crisis.

The National Anthem was sung at the close of the service.

Issue; Saturday, 17th August, 1918.

Pacifists and Cowards:

"Sir, In your issue of 10th inst., Rev. Mr. Muirhead is reported as saying that "there were in that midst" men who called themselves - - - but always there were cowards." Presuming that he is accurately reported, bold justice to the brave demands that that gross lie be refuted. There is in the ranks of the few pacifists of Stra'ven at least one who possesses a certificate of bravery on life-saving under exceptional circumstances, and many of Mr Muirhead's audience on 4th inst., must have been present on the occasion of its presentation from a public platform. They certainly did not evince a desire to restrain their applause then. Have the pacifists a right to ask if there was in Mr Muirhead's audience one who holds a certificate of bravery in the taking of life.

Signed: Pacifist."

Issue: Saturday, 24th August, 1918.

Motor Accidents:

Robert Steel, blacksmith, Commercial Road, met with an accident about 3 pm on Saturday last in Darvel Road, below Bent Farm, by a passing motor car. He was injured on the breast, and bruised the right hand, legs and back. On 15th inst., about 4 pm, while John Irvine, Insurance Agent, was cycling in Townhead Street, he collided with a motor car, and was thrown to the ground, receiving fracture of the right shoulder blades.

War Fund Exposition and Sports:

The committee of the Merchant's Association recommend that shops should be closed today from twelve to five.

War Relief Fund Exposition:

The event of the season takes place today in the West Overton Park in aid of the War Relief Fund. Grand exposition, fancy dress parade, and free gift sale. Don't miss this treat.

Treat for Wounded Soldiers:

The Bowling Club have arranged to entertain a party of about 40 wounded soldiers from Hillpark Auxiliary Hospital. The club hopes that a large number of ladies and gentlemen will be present to welcome the guests.

Accident:

On 15th inst., about 4 p.m., while John Irvine, insurance agent, was cycling in Townhead Street, he collided with a motor car, and was thrown to the ground, receiving fracture of the right shoulder blade.

Mentioned in Dispatches:

Captain A. C. Jennings, Army Service Corps, mentioned in dispatches in "London Gazette" of the 13th inst., for valuable services rendered in connection with the war, is the second son of Captain R. Jennings, M.C., Hayfield, Strathaven, who has four sons serving at the present time in the Army. He himself was awarded the Military Cross for distinguished services in the field. and has been twice mentioned in dispatches.

Football Committee's Effort:

In connection with the sports and football match held during the Fair week the Committee of the Strathaven Caley Football Club held a meeting on Monday evening, 22nd July, to audit the books. They have much pleasure in announcing that the total sum, after deducting expenses, to be handed over to the Operetta Committee amounted to about £61. The donations given by local gentlemen came to about £20, all of which was utilised for prizes, expenses, &c. The committee regret that this announcement has been so long delayed, but the fault was not entirely theirs. They have also to thank the gentlemen who so generously gave donations.

Pacifists and Cowards:

"Sir, - Your report of my address in so far as quoted by your correspondent "Pacifist" in your issue of 17th curt. is correct. What I have said. I have said. To me the issue is quite clear. If in Strathaven we were suddenly overwhelmed by an invader; our women folk murdered after being subjected to horrors worse than death itself; our children, innocent of wrong, wantonly slaughtered before our eyes; our elders and councillors set against the wall and shot because they murmured against such unheard of ferocity - if these things had happened in Strathaven, is there a man worthy of the name of manhood who would not at once fly to arms, or do all in his power to punish the miscreants? But if unhappily there were such an one, what terms of scorn and reproach could be strong enough to hurl at him. Now sir, all these horrors have been perpetuated elsewhere, and very many more besides. Think of Belgium, of Serbia, of Roumania, of Armenia and then its murdered people; think of the bombing of Red Cross hospitals and the slaughter of helpless wounded men; think of the machine guns turned upon defenceless nurses fleeing for refuge; of liquid fire poured upon the wounded prisoners of our own Royal Highlanders; try and picture in your mind say one of these barbarous crimes - all of them contrary to International Law - then is not your amazement and horror and indignation intensified tenfold, when you discover that there are men cowardly enough to seek to make peace with an enemy utterly unrepentant, and utterly devoid of the noblest attributes of humanity - reverence for plighted word, compassion for the weak, mercy for the fallen, and pity for the wounded. Sir, "bold justice to the brave" indeed demands something - not a pitifully weak and inconsistently anonymous letter exclaiming against the name of coward as applied to pacifist, but rather instant action on their part in joining up with those who know that the only enduring peace is to be obtained by caging the savage beast that is rampaging through Europe, and in rendering it

impossible for him to murder and destroy any more. In this way pacifists may purge the stain, and render justice to the brave men who have suffered and died for even such as they are, and also secure that not in vain has courageous and noble blood been shed. Apologising for taking up your space -

I am, etc., J Muirhead, The Manse, Strathaven, 20/8/18

Issue: Saturday, 31st August, 1918.

Croix De Guerre:

Major D. Dougal, M.D., M.C., R.A.M.C., of 11 John Street, Manchester, son of Dr. James Dougal, late of Strathaven, has just been awarded the French decoration the Croix De Guerre, with palms for distinguished service at the front. He has been over three years in France.

Pacifists and Cowards:

"Sir, - In my letter of 18th inst., "bold" should have read "bald justice." The Rev. Muirhead's letter is simply an extension of the theme of his "sermon" to which I took no exception. He very carefully ignores my complaint and challenge and sets himself above the statutes of the realm, which recognise and legalise the claims of certain persons for instance, ministers of religion to exemption from military service. He insulted a brave man whom Strathaven, a year or so ago took delight in honouring, and I submit that as the facts are no longer in question through his admission that "what he has said he has said." the only honourable course is a dignified apology. I have no desire to follow Mr Muirhead in the subject matter of his letter, at least in the columns of your valuable medium, which minister to more desirable purposes, nor to minimise the horrors of the atrocities, which are ever the accompaniments of organised warfare (our Prime Minister was mobbed in Manchester for denouncing the atrocities of the Boer War), but I am glad my moral code was inculcated in Strathaven many years before Mr Muirhead became parish minister. The traditional function of clergymen through the ages has been to restrain the violence of men, not to inflame them. There is no place in a Christian minister's dictionary for such words as "punish" or "avenge". A greater than Mr Muirhead has "said what He has said," and I respectfully suggest that at the next commemoration day he should choose this for his text: "Vengeance is mine, saith the Lord: I will repay." And as my desire for anonymity has been misconstrued, I have pleasure in signing myself ANDREW FLEMING ("A Stra'ven Callant.") 384 Main Street, Shettleston. Glasgow."

Issue: Saturday, 7th September, 1918.

Accident:

On Monday last, at Craigthorn Farm, Glassford, while corn was being cut, the two-and-a-half year old daughter of Matthew Stewart, inmate of the farm, wandered in among the corn, and got in front of the knife. Her foot was cut off below the knee. She was attended by Dr. Petrie, from Strathaven, and afterwards removed to the Infirmary at Glasgow, where she was operated on.

Issue: Saturday, 14th September, 1918.

Cadets:

The Strathaven Company of the 1st Battalion Lanarkshire Cadets had a church parade to the Parish Church on Sunday last, Lieutenant Munro in command. The cadets marched from the school to the church, where the front seats were reserved for them. The Rev. J. Muirhead, in speaking to his text, "Fight the Good Fight," said that the cadets were part of the future hope of Strathaven, and they should not only learn to fight by force of arms, but also to Fight the Good Fight of Faith. After the service the cadets were inspected by Mr Muirhead.

Life Guards:

The inauguration of the life-saving guards took place in the S.A. Hall on Monday, and a very large audience was present. Major Webber presented the registration certificate to Ensign Spence, and appointed her as the commanding officer of the troop, and Captain Middleton as singer instructor. Miss M. Marshall was commissioned as guard leader, her assistant being Miss M. Lindsay; Miss L. Allen, as guard chaplain, Miss M. Moffat, drill instructor, Miss A. White, sewing instructor. Guards Marshall and Baxter were also appointed as corporals. A grand programme was rendered by the guards, including recitations, duets, first-aid exercises in bandaging, dumb-bell drill, and dialogues.

Issue: Saturday, 21st September, 1918.

Scottish Women's Recruiting Work:

Attention is directed to the advertisements appearing on another page. Forms of application and particulars may be obtained from the local agent of the Unemployment Fund, Mr A. Wilson, 32 Kirk Street,.

Army Honour to an Academy Medallist:

The many friends of Corporal Wm. Watson, R.E., will be delighted to learn that he has been awarded the Distinguished Conduct Medal for bravery in taking charge of a dangerous survey post which he resolutely retained during an action that extended over a week. Mr. Watson was Dux Medallist of Strathaven Academy in 1910. He then proceeded to Allan Glen's. Glasgow, and later on to the university, where after a distinguished career he graduated B.Sc.

Academy Cadet Company:

With the kind permission of Captain Napier of Lethame, the Academy Cadet Company, under the command of Lieutenant Munro, assisted by Sergeant Major Kennedy, was allowed to carry out certain manoeuvres in the large field adjoining his house on Friday evening. These were executed with a precision that indicated careful training. At the close Captain Napier inspected the company, congratulated the boys on their efficiency, and expressed the hope that many more would soon enrol and thus form a strong company. Thereafter, the boys were entertained to tea by Mrs Miller, Lethame, in front of the house. A hearty vote of thanks was given to Captain Napier, and Mrs Miller, on the call of Mr Miller, headmaster, who is honorary captain of the company.

Issue: Saturday, 28th September, 1918.

Anniversary Services:

As will be seen from our advertising column, anniversary services are to be held in the East Church on Sabbath first. The preacher this year is the Rev. W.J. Street, M.A., of Glasgow, formerly of Dumfries and latterly of London. Mr Street is one of the newer accession to the preachers of Glasgow and has already won a large place for himself. In view of the increasing congregational expenditure, the managers of the church are asking for a specially large collection on the occasion of these services.

Issue: Saturday, 11th October, 1918.

Sergeant Kennedy:

Sergeant Major Kennedy has resumed his duties as Drill Instructor of boys, his war duties having been completed.

Issue: Saturday, 19th October, 1918.

University Passes:

Miss Jean Riddell, Kirk Street, and Mr Alan Watt McRorie, West Manse, are amongst the list of passes at the university. Miss Riddell has obtained the degree of M.A., and Mr McRorie has passed as M.B., Ch.B., with distinction in midwifery.

Issue: Saturday, 26th October, 1918.

Military Cross:

Captain William Hamilton, M.B., Ch. B., R.A.M.C., now on active service in France, has been awarded the Military Cross. He is the eldest son of the late William Hamilton and Mrs Hamilton, Logan Bank, Strathaven.

Schools Closed:

Owing to the epidemic of influenza, the School Board thought it advisable to close the school. It was closed on Thursday, 17th October, for the Autumn Holiday, and it was announced from the pulpits last Sunday that it was to remain closed for a fortnight. Acting in co-operation with the School Board, the Sabbath Schools have also been closed for a fortnight.

Prisoners of War:

Private John Wright, Scottish Rifles, reported prisoner of war at Friedrichsfeid, Germany, is well known in Motherwell, and is a member of a family that has given many sons to the services. He was at one time employed in the Burgh Lighting Department, and previous to enlistment was with the British Welding Company. His wife and family reside at 19 Baillie's Sq - Private David Brown, Northumberland Fusiliers reported prisoner at the same camp in Germany, has been on service for 3 years. He enlisted when 19, and is 22 years of age this week. Before joining up Private Brown was a baker with the Dalziel Co-operative Society. His parents reside at 59 Manse Road.

Issue: Saturday, 9th November, 1918.

Grateful Belgians:

"Madame De Moor and myself wish to thank the Belgian Committee and the many friends for the kindness and hospitality which we have received since, as refugees, we arrived in Strathaven. In returning to Belgium we will always cherish the memory of our stay here, and will always remember with deep gratitude the kindness, consideration and sympathy received at the hands of the Strathaven people. - Cyril De Moor."

End of the War - Peace with Victory:

"The strife is o'er, the battle done." The Allies have finished their task. At five o'clock French time on the morning of Monday, 11th November, Germany, through her representatives within the French lines, signed the armistice drawn up by the Allied Powers, and hostilities ceased at eleven o'clock forenoon of the same day. *"I have waited for this hour,"* said Mr Lloyd George on Saturday evening, and a famous London editor, who has served the nation splendidly, and who never doubted the same, expressed the hope in the darkest days of the conflict that God would spare him . . . such a moment as this. Both have been rewarded in a measure beyond even their happiest imaginings. The end has come. It is complete, decisive, crushing. After four years and fully three months of the greatest struggle in history, the Allies have seen the whole fabric of Central European administration, with all its vaunting ambition and tyrannical power, crumble to pieces, its crowns and thrones shattered by hammer blows from . . . revolution within. And who will pity the fate of those empires whose rulers set out to achieve unlimited power and domination in goose-stepping over their neighbours? They have sown the wind - they reap the whirlwind. The deliverance which has been wrought by the Allied armies and navies vibrates throughout the world. It is the prelude of a greater moment than that which was in the mind of Wordsworth when he wrote -

"Bliss was it at that dawn to be alive."

The ideal of President Wilson - to make the world free for democracy - is taking practical shape more rapidly than the most sanguine could have dreamt. *"The sea-winds,"* as Whittier said of another great occasion, *"are burdened with the sound of falling chains."* The Continental peoples who were recently our enemies are now discovering that the long drawn out struggle was really a battle for their own deliverance from an oppressive military system which, carried to its extreme, as it was by the Prussian Junkers, could only lead to disaster and disintegration. Nemesis has fallen on that system. Thanks to the courage and endurance of the Allied forces on sea and land the lesson has been driven home to the heart of the Central Powers with almost staggering exactitude and completeness. The Prussian beast has not merely been scotched. It has been slain outright. The haughty and arrogant head of the Hohenzollern's with his *"frown and wrinkled lip and sneer of cold command,"* is now a fugitive from his own people in an alien land, and with him there passes from the world the unholy doctrine that the State is supreme and that its might is right, subject neither to law nor reason. It is, with a deep sense of gratitude that the nation pays tribute to all who have fought and suffered and died to achieve for civilisation the precious boon of an abiding peace, unmenaced by the selfish aggression of such supreme war lords as have just been driven from their exalted pedestals. If the rejoicing has been less demonstrative than on many lesser occasions in our history it is because the joy is more deeply felt. It has been restrained by sorrow. It is true again, as Mrs Browning wrote of the day of Marathon -

"Thro' the wide shores resound triumphant cries,

Fill all the seas, and thunder thro' the skies."

But we think also of the non-returning brave in ever grateful memory do we hold them. While we mourn their loss they, indeed, have made it possible for us to thank God that *"We mourn no blighted hope nor broken plan."* Long deferred, our hope has been gloriously realised - the plan has been magnificently completed. The mad Moloch of Europe has been destroyed beyond the possibility of recovery, and the world sees with a great sense of relief that on his impious altars no more human sacrifices will be necessary. The war interrupted and finally extinguished the well laid plans of many promising lives, on whose graves in distant lands and under the wide seas the silent stars look down. But they helped to complete a greater plan - a plan for the world and for the ages to come, and theirs too, are the crown and the victory. Lanarkshire's contribution to the victory is one of which the county has reason to be proud. Its expenditure in men, money, and material has been worthy of its position. From its steel and coal industries have gone forth day by day those munitions that forged the way to victory. For these past four years the incessant glow of the furnaces have reddened the evening sky, producing a never-lifting cloud of smoke by day and a pillar fire by night. The men who sweated and toiled in producing the essential things without which the triumph could not have been secured deserve our gratitude also. And we cannot forget the very important and altogether remarkable part which women have taken in these industries, where their aid has been indispensable. In money to carry on the war, and for relief and Red Cross purposes, the county has not failed. Unstintedly it has given of its treasures in response to every call for mashing the "silver bullets" to help with the war, and the golden gifts to soften and ameliorate its sufferings. And shall it ever be possible to tabulate the immense amount of voluntary work undertaken by those at home, but particularly by the women folk, whose nimble and loving and unceasingly industrious fingers wrought those countless garments and comforts designed to give our soldiers comfort and our wounded ease. "Oh it's a lovely war," sang our soldiers as they ploughed their way through the mud of Flanders with the rain dripping from their steel helmets. As one they cheerfully made light of their hardships they unconsciously gave expression to what everyone must feel has been of incalculable power and value throughout the long travail of war. The love and sacrifice poured out have been superb, and this outpouring sustained the hearts of our men through all their trials and sufferings. Finally, there was the country's contribution in men for the combatant services. That also shows a magnificent record of sacrifice and heroism. Who, having witnessed it, can forget the rush of men to Hamilton from all parts of the county when the news came during those dark days of August and early September, 1914, of the sad gaps in the ranks of the valiant and glorious "Old Contemptibles," faced by foes numbering five to one." Every train to Hamilton poured out its stream of men till the Barracks and the Territorial headquarters at Motherwell were literally stormed with volunteers eager to step into the breach. Centres were improvised for enrolment, and recruiting clerks, facing the crowds of Lanarkshire youths, whose eyes already glistened with the prospect of the Great Adventure shouted - *"All for the Black Watch this way," "Who's for the Argylls?" "Here . . . For the Bnffs"; "Now, then, round here for the Gordons,"* and every clerk was besieged. At long last the volunteer stream faded, or at any rate trickled so slowly as to place our forces in the field in peril. First the Derby scheme was put into operation, but finally the conscription of the nation's fit manhood became imperative. By whatever means the men from Lanarkshire went forth to battle with the enemy, and they have nobly and heroically played their part in the stupendous achievement of decisive victory.

Peace Rejoicing:

The news that the armistice had been signed reached Strathaven at about 11.35 and immediately the church bells rung out a gladsome peal. People thronged into the Parish Church where a brief service of thanksgiving was conducted by the Rev. John Muirhead, B.D., assisted by the Rev. T.M. Dey, B.D., and Matthew Urie Baird, M.A. The church was full of people who had suddenly left their work and joined in the service. It was a novel and delightful sight to see men fresh from the anvil, and women from the loom, in their working garb crowding into the House of God to give thanks. After the benediction, the congregation flocked to the Commongreen, and joined heartily in the 100th Psalm and the National Anthem. Thereafter, hearty cheers were given for the Navy, the Army, and the Avondale men who had gone forth. At eight o'clock in the evening a more formal service was held in the Parish Church, conducted by the Revs. J. Muirhead, T.M. Dey, and M. Urie Baird. The building was packed to overflowing, Besides the ordinary congregation, there was a full turnout of the Academy Cadets under Lieutenant Munro; the Boys' Brigade, under Lieutenant Johnstone, the

Salvation Army, Girl Guides, and the local orchestra under Mr R. Leggate. Proceedings opened with the 53rd Psalm. Mr Dey then engaged in a prayer of thanksgiving. Mr Baird read the lessons from Psalm 85 and Romans 8, verse 31 to end. Paraphrase 66 was sung between the Old Testament and New Testament portions. After the congregation had rendered Psalm 124, the 2nd version, with great heartiness, a stirring address was given by Mr Muirhead, who chose as his subject, "The Victory - its Price and its Fruit," basing his remarks on 1 Chronicles xxix., 11 - *"Thine, o Lord, is the greatness, and the power, and the victory, and the majesty,"* - and 1 John verse 4 - *"This is the victory that overcometh the world, even your faith."* After divine service, a huge bonfire was lit on Kirkhill in the presence of a great crowd, who cheered to the echo of the words of the minister that the just judgement of God had descended upon a cruel and brutal foe who had aimed at world demunion, but who had succumbed to the triumphant powers of righteousness. All night rejoicing people made merry in the Market Place with great good humour and heartiness.

Issue: Saturday, 30th November, 1918

War Honour:

Friends of Second Lieutenant Andrew Hamilton, Manchester Regiment, youngest son of Mr James Hamilton, Cheese Merchant, will be pleased to learn that under date 16th inst., he has been awarded the Military Cross for bravery in the field. Lieutenant A. Hamilton joined the Royal Scots in November, 1914, as a private, and with that regiment saw two years service in France, taking part in the Somme offensive. In April of this year he obtained his commission, and was wounded during the recent fighting in front of Le Cateau. He is now progressing favourably.

Issue: Saturday, 21st December, 1918

A Grand Entertainment and Treat:

A grand entertainment and treat under the auspices of the Scottish Federation of Discharged and Demobilised Sailors and Soldiers, is advertised to be given in the Public Hall, Uddingston and Bothwell on Tuesday next. Names of dependants who may have been overlooked should be sent in at once to Barnet McIntosh, secretary, The Laundry, Bellshill Road, Uddingston.

Avondale War Relief Fund:

At a meeting of the Executive Committee on Monday night, - Mr James Cameron in the chair, - there was a unanimous feeling that some form of memorial should be gone on with. At a previous meeting various schemes had been suggested and it was now agreed, also unanimously, that a public meeting should be held in the Public Hall on Monday first (as advertised) to decide as to the raising of funds.

Issue: 28th December, 1918.

Obituary:

The remains of Pte. David Graham, Highland Light Infantry, were interred in the New Cemetery on Thursday. Pte. Graham was a pre-war soldier, having enlisted in the Dragoon Guards when a lad. Shortly before the outbreak of the war he was transferred in India to the Highland Light Infantry, and with that battalion he came to France in 1914. Very soon after their arrival the battalion had a disastrous experience, in which Pte. Graham was supposed to have been killed. Later, however, he wrote from a German internment camp intimating that he was a prisoner. The signing of the armistice brought his return, but he was only able to reach this country when he collapsed, and had to be taken to hospital, where he died of pneumonia. There was a large attendance of soldiers on furlough, returned prisoners, corps cadets, and Boys' Brigade at the funeral, in addition to a great number of civilians. Revs. J. Muirhead, and T. M. Dey conducted the service at the house, and Rev. James McRorie at the graveside. Pte. Graham was 28 years of age. Much sympathy is felt for his widowed mother, who resides at 3 Kirk Street.

This memorial to the honoured memory of the men of Avondale who fell in The Great War 1914 - 1918 was unveiled and dedicated on Kirkhill on Saturday, 3rd June, 1922. That day there was held a Divine Service in the Parish Church at 2.45 p.m. and, thereafter, a march to Kirkhill headed by the band of the 1st Battalion Royal Scots Fusiliers for the unveiling ceremony. The unveiling was performed by Mrs Lee Dykes, East Overton, and the Address given by Lt.-General Sir Francis J. Davies, K.C.B., K.C.M.G., K.C.V.O., A.D.A., Commander-in-Chief of the Forces in Scotland. The band played the lament, 'The Flowers o' the Forest'. The memorial was handed over to the care of the Parish Council by James Barrie, J.P., and custody accepted by John Bertram, Esq., J.P., Chairman of the Council. The memorial now also commemorates the men of Avondale who fell in the Second World War 1939 - 1945. The memorial is now in the care of South Lanarkshire Council. An annual service of remembrance, led by members of the British Legion, is held at the War Memorial on the Sunday nearest the eleventh day of November at the eleventh hour.

It's Only a Penny
by
Don Drew

Many people alive today will retain childhood memories of barrel organs playing by the kerbside in the streets of our towns and cities. Don Drew has one particular recollection, which has remained with him ever since that moment in the late 1920s. He was only a little lad at the time, clutching his mother's hand as she went shopping along the busy Ilford High Road, and on that day he remembers hearing 'jingly' music, and then coming upon three shabbily-dressed men,

one of them turning the handle of a barrel organ. He recalls their cloth caps looking too large for them because of their sunken cheeks. With hindsight, he now supposes they were plain hungry.

Those were hard times. It was much, much later that he came to realise that what they had pinned to their worn-out jackets were frayed medal ribbons.

Don's mum - always a soft touch - put a copper or two into the grubby cap which one of the men held out, to receive a muttered "Thanks you, Lady". When Don gave her a questioning look, she explained, saying (in words that echo down the years), *They're old soldiers who fought for us in the*

War". Reliving the moment, it comes over strongly to Don that his mother must have been motivated by the death of her own brother in that terrible conflict, then but ten years before.

Don remembers his widowed grandmother as a little woman with silver hair in a bun and with skirts that touched down to the floor. He recalls that he never saw her wear anything but black. A link with her dead soldier son of twenty-four was a round bronze plaque which stood on her sideboard, displayed on its own little easer. He says "I think it was that easel - a miniature of the blackboard easel at school - which as a child probably fascinated me most". Some eighty years later, that same plaque is now in Don's care, It's pictured here inscribed with the full name of the man who would have become his Uncle Fleetwood.

Fleetwood George Bolitho had been an infantryman in The Rifle Brigade, and a few years ago Don made a pilgrimage to his grave which is in one of the smaller war cemeteries in France, and quite close to the scene of his death. It was a lovely September day, and so unbelievably still and peaceful.

Don looked into the history of these memorial plaques, and it's an interesting one. It was as early as 1916 that the proposal for them came about. The euphoria of August 1914, with its flag-waving and cries of *"Home by Christmas"*, was but a memory. And the lengthening casualty lists spoke eloquently of the true cost. The names of the World War One fallen which are to be seen on war memorials right across the land express how strongly the loss of those young men impacted upon local communities in Britain's villages, towns and cities in the years that followed their deaths.

And 1916 had not been an auspicious year. There had been the Easter Rising in Dublin, and then, in May, the Battle of Jutland, a momentous engagement in the North Sea with no conclusive outcome - although the German High Seas Fleet was never again to put to sea. It is still remembered by many for the posthumous award of the Victoria Cross to 16 year old Jack Cornwell (see footnote), who was the sight-setter on the vulnerable fc'sle gun of the cruiser HMS Chester. Barely a month, after came the great Somme offensive, with 60,000 British casualties on the very first day. So at a time when the prospect of continued conflict must have stretched distantly ahead, there was this inspiration to provide for those individual permanent memorials for the fallen.

The proposal was made public with *The Times* headline of 7ᵗʰ November 1916, which read: *Memento for the Fallen. State Gift for Relatives*. A committee was set up to progress the idea, in which both Houses of Parliament were represented, together with the War Office, the Admiralty, Colonial Office, India Office, and the Dominions. Artistic input was provided by the British Museum, the V & A and the National Gallery.

The way forward was decided to be by way of public competition, and this was announced in the following August. The commemoration was to be in the form of a bronze plaque, and a symbolic figure with the wording "HE DIED FOR FREEDOM AND HONOUR" were to form an integral part of the design. There was a prize fund of £500; a quite magnificent sum, which amounts to some £25,000 in 2010.

Over 800 entries were received, and the first prize of £250 was awarded to Mr Edward Carter Preston of Sandon Studios Society, Liverpool. His winning circular design comprised the figure of Britannia, robed and helmeted, holding a laurel wreath and supporting a trident, with a male lion in the foreground. On either side of Britannia's shoulders there was a dolphin, representing Britain's sea-power. The required words of dedication bordered half of the plaque, and the artist's initials appeared by the lion's right fore-paw. At the base of the design there was a small depiction of a lion slaying an eagle, which represented the destruction of the Central Powers.

To accompany each plaque sent to the next-of kin there was to be a letter from the King, together with a Memorial Scroll. The King had taken a close personal interest in the whole project and his letter read:

I join with my grateful people

in sending you this memorial

of a brave life given for others

in the Great War.

The wording of the Memorial Scroll created quite a challenge. To quote from Philip Dutton's history of the plaques: *"The minds of the contemporary literary world were ransacked in an effort to obtain a satisfactory elegiac formula"*. In the event, though, Dr Montague Rhodes James, Provost of King's College, Cambridge, was approached, and he sent a draft "by return of post"! His wording reads most movingly:

He whom this scroll commemorates

Was numbered among those who,

At the call of King and Country, left all

That was dear to them, endured hardness,

Faced danger; and finally passed out of

The sight of men by the path of duty

And self-sacrifice, giving up their own

Lives that others might live in freedom.

Let those who come after see to it

That his name be not forgotten.

Reflect for a moment upon the elegance of the phrase "... finally passed out of the sight of men by the path of duty and self-sacrifice ..." Such sentiments ring somewhat strangely in our ears today, but all those years ago attitudes and standards were very different. The mood of the time is captured well by Deborah Lake, where she writes in her book of the men of the Royal Navy and Royal Marines who *"fought because of patriotism and a belief in the King and their Country ... They had ungrudging valour and a fierce sense of duty."*

Production of the plaques began in December 1918, each one an individual casting with the name appearing in full. The British sense of humour, with more than a flavour of irony, dubbed the plaques "Death Pennies" or "Widows' pennies, hence the title of this piece.

One wonders, where are all those million-or-so plaques? Some are in museums or collections, but most must still be with the families. If you have one, you might like to enter the name on the search website of the Commonwealth War Graves Commission - www.cwgc.org.uk, where there is information of the dates of death of all casualties, and the cemeteries where they lie or the places of commemoration of those with no known grave.

These plaques are nowadays within the province of collector5s, and any bearing the name of a woman (some 600 were issued for nurses and service-women), or particularly of a VC, can command high prices. They are occasionally on offer at car boot sales and if you see one there then do pick it up and for a moment think of the man or woman it commemorates, who was one of those from Britain and the Dominions to fall in that tragic conflict we call The Great War.

And do remember, too, the grieving mothers and wives who first received these plaques. There would also have been more than a million of them . . . Women who had borne the wartime hardships at home and brought up families, while fearing all the time for their distant loved ones serving the fight on land, sea and in the air. We are surely indebted to them.

WITH GRATEFUL ACKNOWLEDGEMENT TO PHILIP DUTTON

AND THE IMPERIAL WAR MUSEUM www.iwm.org.uk

AND ALSO TO HERBERT G SMART FOR HIS 1983 ACCOUNT.

John Travers Cornwell VC had been a Boy Scout, and he is commemorated in perpetuity by The Cornwell Badge, which was instituted by The Scout Association in recognition of his exemplary conduct that day in May 1916. The badge is awarded to Scouts who have displayed pre-eminently high character, devotion to duty, together with courage and endurance. Alec Tobin, a Patrol Leader of the 1st Carmarthen Scout Troop, aged 15, was awarded the badge in March 1940, for his great and lasting fortitude during many years of eye surgery, from the time he was a small child.